LEADING with LOVE and LAUGHTER

LEADING with LOVE and LAUGHTER

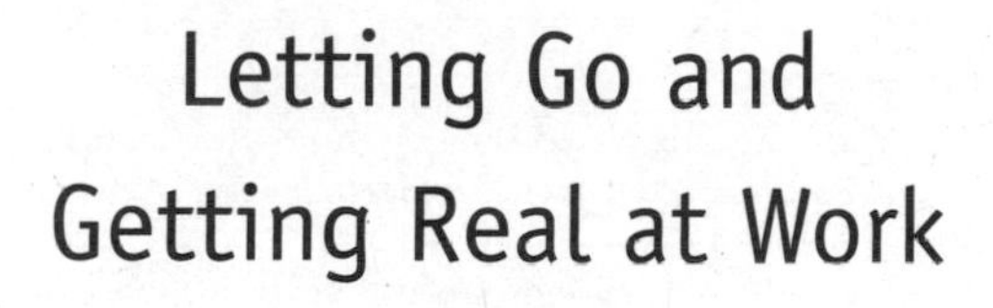

Letting Go and Getting Real at Work

Zina Sutch
and
Patrick Malone

Berrett–Koehler Publishers, Inc.

Berrett-Koehler Publishers, Inc.
1333 Broadway, Suite 1000
Oakland, CA 94612-1921
Tel: (510) 817-2277
Fax: (510) 817-2278
www.bkconnection.com

ORDERING INFORMATION
Quantity sales. Special discounts are available on quantity purchases by corporations, associations, and others. For details, contact the "Special Sales Department" at the Berrett-Koehler address above.
Individual sales. Berrett-Koehler publications are available through most bookstores. They can also be ordered directly from Berrett-Koehler: Tel: (800) 929-2929; Fax: (802) 864-7626; www.bkconnection.com.
Orders for college textbook / course adoption use. Please contact Berrett-Koehler: Tel: (800) 929-2929; Fax: (802) 864-7626.

Distributed to the U.S. trade and internationally by Penguin Random House Publisher Services.

Printed in Canada

Berrett-Koehler books are printed on long-lasting acid-free paper. When it is available, we choose paper that has been manufactured by environmentally responsible processes. These may include using trees grown in sustainable forests, incorporating recycled paper, minimizing chlorine in bleaching, or recycling the energy produced at the paper mill.

Cataloging-in-Publication Data is available at the Library of Congress.
Library of Congress Control Number: 2021930304
ISBN: 978-1-5230-9321-2

First Edition

27 26 25 24 23 22 21 10 9 8 7 6 5 4 3 2 1

Book producer and text designer: Leigh McLellan. Author photo: Bill Petros.
Cover designer: Nola Burger. Copyeditor: Elissa Rabellino.
Proofreader: Mary Hazlewood. Indexer: Ken DellaPenta.

For Lidia and Billie Faye . . .

CONTENTS

PREFACE

Anyone picking up this book might be wondering not only why this topic and why now, but also who these authors are and what brought them together to write this book. Like they say on Facebook, it's complicated. No, not really. We think there is a set of core beliefs that we both share, and some would argue that these beliefs were being cultivated our entire lives. When we were brought together through a series of professional and personal events, it felt as if we had found our purpose—we saw our future filled with, you guessed it, love and laughter. We will share how this book was born in the introduction, but for now, let's talk about the least important thing in this book—us. LOL.

We were both born into loving families, and for much of our childhoods we experienced many challenges. One of us is the daughter of two immigrants who came to this country with their families in their late teens, found each other in New England, served in the armed forces, and started their own family. The other was born in Texas to parents whose roots in America, from what we can tell, date back to the early 1800s. Both of us share common threads in our upbringing; we both began with meager means and tight budgets, doing without all of the latest and greatest things, yet occasionally we were treated to gifts such as a guitar or piano and music lessons. These gifts, we recognized at a young age, came from our parents' sacrifices and exceptional work ethic, for which we are both so very grateful. We learned early on that we might not have had what everyone else had, but we had families that struggled and fortunately made it. In one of our families, love and laughter were evident and observable, demonstrative and expressive. In the other, love and laughter were a bit more reserved, expressed on a more personal level and quietly, without fanfare. Yet we both felt loved and experienced joy.

We were each the first in our family to earn a doctoral degree, and for one of us this was while serving in the U.S. Navy for twenty-three years and raising three daughters. For the other, the degree was earned over ten years while working in public service full time and raising two daughters. Yes, that makes for a handful of amazing daughters between us.

What we share are a belief in the importance of serving others, especially those less fortunate; the ability to empathize with others in difficult situations; the need for kindness and compassion in our everyday lives; the belief that every individual has value; and many more along these lines. These ideals brought us individually to the Key Executive Leadership Programs at American University, one as the director of the programs, the other as a student and eventually a faculty member. This is where, through classroom dialogue and much discussion, our personal and professional connection was formed. We learned how much we already shared, how passionate we both were about the same things, and how much we could do working together. We both teach leadership development in these programs, and after numerous conversations and similar observations, we knew we had something to offer and a new path to forge.

We did not do this work alone. There are so many we want to acknowledge who influenced us and were the reason we came together, learned together, and wrote together.

First, we must thank Don Zauderer, founder of the Key Executive Leadership Programs, and the reason we met. He had the vision, the understanding, and the chutzpah to challenge the way leaders are developed. Don brought cohorts together and nurtured leaders to build loving relationships with each other before they ever read a book or learned a best practice. We also gratefully acknowledge Karlease Kelly, who was the supervisor that recommended an approach with "an open heart," which you will read about in the introduction. She started us on this path of using words that are uncommon in the workplace. She is the consummate human leader. Smart, caring, loving. Thank you, Karlease.

Much love and appreciation to our colleagues who support, teach, and coach in the Key Executive Leadership Programs. They exhibit love and laughter every day, whether it be in the classroom, one-on-one, or with one another. You are the best there is at uncovering leadership talent, and we love and respect all of you.

We also want to thank all of the great leaders for whom we have worked that showed us what to do, what not to do, how to love, and how to laugh: Rosalind H., Beth, Jeff, Karlease, Mark, Mr. Spurck, Raquel, Vicky, Linda, Dave, and any we've missed. You all have touched us, inspired us, and made us the leaders we are. Thank you for your love when we needed it, and the laughter timed just perfectly.

Leading people is a lot like creating a work family. There are joy and tears, fun and fears. Thank you to our kids for teaching us to laugh and love in ways we never thought possible.

We are thankful for Susan Hopp, Sally Anlin, and Scott Gassman, our reviewers, who took our initial manuscript and thoughtfully provided us with guidance on how to make our message clearer. We read every word and contemplated every recommendation.

A huge shout-out to our sailing and boating friends at Herrington Harbour, in North Beach, Maryland. You all have been so very kind to us, sustaining friendships even when we responded to invitations with "Sorry! We have to work on the book and can't hang out this weekend." Thank you for still being our shipmates!

Speaking of our home marina, we want to acknowledge owner Steuart Cheney of Herrington Harbour North and Herrington Harbour South on the Chesapeake Bay. He is a leader who exhibits humility, humor, and love. He has created a place of peace, inclusion, and solace that gave us the perfect environment in which to craft this book.

So we're just going to say it. We would be remiss if we did not note that we sit in awe of Neal Maillet, who was willing to meet with us to discuss an idea we had about a book on leadership. His enthusiasm and belief in our work was worth every day and every hour that it took to write. We were able to believe in ourselves because Neal believed in us and the subject of this book. The three of us immediately recognized how essential this topic is and how important this work could be for the field of leadership. Through multiple transcontinental Zoom meetings, we honed the idea of how one must tap into that deeper self to find the love and the laughter that make us human. The day we agreed on a title for the work is still etched in our hearts as one of the most joyful days of our lives. Thanks for believing in us, Neal.

As a final note, we want to say that we continue to experience love and laughter in our lives. Living on a sailboat forces us to recognize the love we have for one another (you can't ever get more than a few feet from each other!) and to laugh at how much we don't know, especially about sailing. The experience of sharing space together in this way has brought us more joy than we can describe. We believe that love and laughter matter, whether one is leading or simply being human. It matters more than we ever knew.

Z & P
s/v Madness

INTRODUCTION

One day, a long, long time ago, two somewhat nerdy, touchy-feely adults, who happened to teach in a pretty cool leadership program, were talking. What were we discussing? one might wonder. We are glad you asked! It was a topic that was often on our minds. Both of us were doing all we could to provide and facilitate leadership development as professors, we both held leadership positions, and we both had experienced successes and failures, as well as the good and the bad, when it came to bosses. It was often entertaining focusing on the bad, but we found ourselves spending a lot of time trying to decipher precisely what it was that was good. What common denominators tended to make leaders successful?

In these discussions, usually over a nice glass of Malbec, we came to the conclusion that something was either there or not there when it came to great leaders. But how to describe it? How to identify it so that we could share it with our students and colleagues? Each conversation continued to revolve around this X factor. We assumed that everyone wanted to be a better leader. They attended trainings, went to seminars, and got degrees. Not all the same ones, mind you, but leader development is common. We surmised that this unknown factor had to be something that everyone was capable of doing. We still believe that.

We kept asking ourselves what was missing in what we were practicing and teaching. We knew there was a feeling one got when in the presence of great leadership and, going even further, when you were in the presence of great people. We started digging deeper into our own practices and how we tried to lead. What was it we asked ourselves daily? What did we say to ourselves when facing difficult situations, difficult times, stressful changes, and failures? One of us had an interesting memory about a supervisor who advised her to approach things with "an open heart." We were onto something. The other replied that he had a mentor who felt that fostering bonds among people was the most important responsibility of a leader. Hmmm, heart? Bonding? Dare we say love? The Malbec was almost gone, but we were close!

Does heart and bonding come into play in most leadership programs? Not so much. We rarely use words that allude to the heart, but we should. We focus too much on scripted approaches to leading and not bonding. So, we knew we weren't there yet. We kept thinking there was more. Then, we put on our serious thinking faces and bingo! That was it! There is usually a seriousness around what we teach and practice. We came to the aha moment when we both recognized that some of the most successful and loved leaders we knew were also fun. They laughed. There is a certain lightheartedness that comes with being real, with showing your human side. This levity can be seen in some of the most highly functioning teams, and it was the second piece of our puzzle.

The picture had taken shape. Love and laughter. We reflected on times when we walked by teams as they were meeting, gathering, or just hanging, and we would hear laughter. We also talked about how there seemed to be joy in the room and unfettered care for one another. These folks loved each other! We realized that some of the best places we had worked had an atmosphere of love and laughter. We also understood that in order for that to exist, the leader had to be in on this, being real, and letting go.

This book was born from these conversations and experiences. We realized that everything we had been teaching with respect to concrete practices, models, and equations was good in theory and even good in practice. However, if a person doesn't recognize and start with the human aspects and human needs for love and laughter, the models will be just that, checklists and practices that don't really do anything except make the leader feel good about his or her investment in leadership development. Start with humanity—that is our message.

Here is the question we've been asking ourselves: Why is it that even when leaders are provided extensive training, understand and implement sophisticated leadership models and approaches, and get trained out the wazoo for any number of leadership skills, they still struggle? Why drop thousands of dollars for THE development program or THE certification at THE school? Why do well-trained leaders still fail? Why do leaders continue faltering at building trust, handling poor performers, or engaging with employees? Why do they settle for having organizations that aren't flourishing? Why is it so hard to lead? What's not working here? OK, so that was more than one question, but you get it.

There are so many leaders out there who are knowledgeable, continuous learners and yearning to get better. You might be that very leader who is looking to grow, steady on your leadership development journey, and tirelessly polishing your leadership proficiencies. You become a disciple of the latest guru and memorize the most current captivating acronym so that you can proclaim your talent as a fill-in-the-blank-with-the-most-current-captivating-acronym leader. There are many organizations out there capitalizing on this phenomenon. They provide certificates, licenses, pathways to "Master" whatever, and anything else the market will bear. While we concede that there may be value to be found in some of these skill-building approaches, there is a serious gap. There must be, because we have leaders in place, credentialed and certified, all over the world, yet we still find that it's not working. Good people, doing good work, using reasonable approaches, checking all the right boxes, and still it feels like something is absent. Something is amiss in the way we have been looking at, thinking about, and, sadly, practicing leadership over the years.

Let's take a look at Margaret, who for all intents and purposes is doing everything right and still getting it wrong:

> Margaret was a seasoned senior leader. She climbed the ladder to professional success having attended all the prominent schools with the names we all recognize, earning certifications in all the popular leadership tools, and finally earning the big promotion. She took over a large organization with visions of excellence, managing a change effort, reskilling employees, and introducing the latest leadership approaches on the organization's path toward success. She arrived amid plenty of fanfare and immediately got to work. She said all the words, checked off the change management boxes, made small talk with employees, walked around the building to shake hands and be seen, held open forums where people could ask questions, and sent out plenty of emails espousing her passion for the people and the organization. Margaret did all the "right" things.
>
> And she failed. Miserably. No one knew her, and most did not know what to make of her. Fewer and fewer employees showed up at her town hall meetings, and those who did asked the same questions, in different ways, in a desperate attempt to figure out who she was and what she was trying to do. Employees were disengaging. She even started walking into the cafeteria and randomly finding people she could sit and chat with (rookie mistake—nobody likes that at lunch!). She did everything she had been taught and followed the script with zeal.
>
> She worked tirelessly to connect with employees, communicate her intentions, and emphasize the benefits of her vision. Her textbook approach and unwavering certainty about leadership as she saw it did not work. She eventually

left with little notice, to an audible sigh of relief from almost everyone in the building. Who was that person?

Margaret committed the classic, mortal leadership sin: She depended on what she had been taught—matrixed models and to-do lists—and trusted that what she had learned made up true leadership. She worshipped at the altar of reports from the big firms, the respected consulting groups who had sold her on leadership development programs that would help her build her leadership skills and abilities. She earned more certificates than could fit on a résumé. And all those initials after her name? There were not enough letters in the alphabet. She had to start using emojis (just kidding).

Many of us do the same as Margaret. We learn, memorize, model, and act the way we were instructed, implementing the techniques we were taught, checking off the boxes as we go. We did it, and you probably did it too. It's easy to hang on acronyms and different-colored belts for achievement. It brings a sense of control and confidence when you rely on tried-and-true practices—or the latest hip endorsements. We feel that we are excelling in the practice of leadership when we can point to a book, an article, a seminar, and say, "Hey, we are doing all of this." The buzzwords are prevalent, meaningful, and easy to remember, and make sense. We believe in these constructs and invest our time and money into expanding our repertoire and our tool kits. However, somehow it doesn't always work. Something is missing—just as we saw in Margaret's example, where the organization just wasn't buying it. What Margaret did was exhaustive and diligent and had all the signs of implementing best practices. So if they were best practices, why didn't they work?

To be fair, formal leadership education can help, a little. These models are often based in solid research and, in some cases, massive surveys and the engagement of statisticians. There is also no shortage of leadership development programs. Some include a walk in the footsteps of historical leaders. These tours are usually through famous battlefields or museum-like presidential homes, retelling leadership stories of famous admirals, CEOs, or presidents. All this in hopes that the leadership lessons are somehow magically absorbed through stories and historical drama. We have even seen leadership programs that teach you how to approach horses, or a prey animal, in a ring. This experience is supposed to help you become more in touch with the emotions you carry and the impact they have on sensitive creatures. OK. So, this may be a unique experience, but we strongly recommend that you check the bottom of your shoes before getting back on the group bus.

In this book, we are not going to focus on what is wrong with organizations and how leaders can fix them. We are not going to focus on what models or equations some use to lead people. Lots of folks have already done this, or claim to. They help clarify organizational issues and provide frameworks for how to make it all better. There is no shortage of these approaches. World-class organizations, authors, and think tanks offer numerous leadership prototypes and accreditations. They frame our thinking and give us guidance. They help us with recipes when we need an outline to follow. And perhaps we can all learn something from experiences in programs such as the above, but that gap we mentioned is still there.

Models will change, theories will come and go, perspectives will vary. Think tanks create new variables, fancy graphics, and complex frameworks every year. Fads come and go, like culottes and bell-bottoms. It's a profit thing, it's a business thing, and it's guaranteed to continue. We encourage all leaders to build their skills and expand their repertoire of techniques. But mind the gap! What will never change are the basic needs that all humans have. Never. Human needs are not vogue. They are forever. Before implementing any of these tools, we need to get to the core of the human need—which, by the way, does not fall by the wayside when we enter our workplace and turn on the computer.

In order for us to benefit from structured instruction and the like, we have to know ourselves first. Leadership begins with our own heart and soul, and those topics don't often make it into the recipe-based leadership approaches so popular today. Our contention is that we must begin with the human self. We cannot successfully lead until we completely understand what is at the core of our own needs as human beings, working alongside other human beings. Once we understand who we are in a complex world, we can then move to the myriad of models and frameworks and proudly wear the T-shirts and carry the insulated coffee mugs that reflect all we have learned about leadership best practices.

The time is now, and the human is you. We're facing a landscape of organizations that are constantly changing—pandemics, artificial intelligence, five generations in the office, and matrixed organizations are just a few of the challenges. New positions are being identified in the workplace that have new names, some of which are quite confusing. An ethical technology adviser, who, get this, evaluates humans and robots on ethical matters. A nostalgist, given the responsibility for being a virtual reality resource for the elderly to return to their days of glory. Or this, a freelance relationships officer. Let's not go there! The reality is that the way things are now is not the way they are going to be five years from now.

What will never, never, never change is our need for love and laughter, our desire to smile and find joy in our lives. This has always been and will always be. Why wouldn't we start there as leaders? Our human hearts and souls will always need connection, bonding, and feel-good hormones that release stress, increasing our commitment and helping us find our purpose in our everyday lives. As leaders, we need to see this desire within ourselves and recognize that our employees, our colleagues, and our own bosses have this need as well. It is forever.

We want to share in this book our views about love and laughter and the critical role they play in leadership. Yes, we will provide examples; yes, we will provide some practices; and yes, we will make you laugh. But we'll do something else first. Before we get to the chapters of the book that tie love and laughter to leadership, we will stick our proverbial toe in the waters of the science and history of what love and laughter really are. The word love is so often used, we forget what it means. Laughter is so often misunderstood and feared that we forget its power in relationships. Once we have a good perspective on what these two phenomena really are, we will apply them directly to our leadership practice, complete with examples of leaders who successfully use love and laughter. We think you will come to admire the four leaders we've chosen as much as we do.

You will see that we use the words *try* and *think* in this book often. It's for a reason. We considered attempting to devise some sort of simple test you could use to foster love and laughter in your leadership and in your life. As you'll read here shortly, it was a tough decision point for us, but we opted against such an approach. There are several problems with faddish self-assessments. Often, they're not scientifically valid—they just look cool. Oh sure, they give us a quick snapshot of something, but how useful is it really? These assessments are also beguiled by a much larger issue: the fact that when we respond to such tools, we respond as we wish ourselves to be, not who we actually are. This leads to the manifestation of the "I got this" leader, whom we introduce in the final chapter.

We've chosen, instead, to ask you to try. Try viewing laughter this way. We ask you to think. Think of the last time you did something or used a particular word. Our suggestions come not from a scripted leadership curriculum but from the science that is love and laughter, and the evidence of the good they can impart in your life and your leadership. They also come from our hearts, with all the good intentions to try to make this world a better place, especially at work. Only you know whether you tried or not, and only you know whether it worked. We trust you.

There's too much certification out there—too many leadership gimmicks that we pay for, seek, and aspire to. We argue for giving yourself certification, a certification in self. This has to come before everything else, for it is the source of great leadership. It takes hard work on a daily or even hourly basis, vulnerability, and self-awareness. It is a beautiful journey, and it will lead to happiness, good health, and success long after the latest leadership craze has come and gone. Truthfully, the answer to leadership has been with us for years: love and laughter. It's a shame that we've lost sight of this. Perhaps it's simply gotten lost in a lot of shiny wrapping paper.

By the way, we promise that, no matter how big this book gets (Pulitzer, Grammy, National Book Award, Nobel, Tony, Oscar), we will not turn this into a certification course. Now, join us on our ascent to heart and humor.

PART I

LOVE

CHAPTER 1

LOVE IS THE ANSWER

Starting the first chapter in a book on leadership with the word *love* is risky business. Here come those mushy soft skills again! But then again, were you not interested, or at least curious, you wouldn't be reading the book anyway, right? We love that you chose to do so. Oops, there's that word again. Love.

The word *love* is used in many different contexts, and we toss the word around like a Frisbee. Most of the time, we use *love* in reference to personal spheres of our lives, our relationships. We build connections with one another and sometimes eventually grow to love each other. We love our partners, our families, our friends. And they love us back. It feels good. But sometimes we love things that don't love us back. This is a more impersonal sphere of love. We love reading. We love burritos. We love burritos (no, our editor did not miss that—we love burritos a lot. It's worth stating twice.). Sometimes we throw up our jazz hands and say, "I love it!" If we aren't the type of person who uses jazz hands, we still feel love.

Yet, when it's used in the context of the workplace, or more specifically the people in our workplace, we shun the notion of love. We say to ourselves, "Wait, what? I can't just exude love to my coworkers and subordinates. I'll look weak. It would be inappropriate. What would they think?" We may say we love our work, and that's equally as meaningful as saying we love burritos, but let's be honest—they *are* burritos after all! So, where does love fit?

Before we tackle these questions, we want to begin by simply making the case for love, because before we can permeate our leadership with love, we need to ground ourselves in an understanding of what love is. And spoiler alert—ten thousand years of philosophical exploration has us no closer to getting a handle on this. It's familiar, maybe too much so, to the point that the word has become almost meaningless. But there are ways for us to envision love, apply it in our daily lives, and be better leaders for it. So, allow us to introduce the notion of love! We say *introduce* because we believe love is something that infuses our lives, yet many still take it for granted. We think we know what love means, how it makes us feel, and that there are many types of love. Let's see what we can uncover.

The Concept of Love

An introduction to the concept of love may seem like a pointless endeavor. Is it worth the presentation of such a common notion? One we all share? If we all know what love is, why the need to introduce it? Because while love may be there in parts of our lives (see partners and burritos above), it's missing in other parts, namely leadership. We generally find love only in places where we feel comfortable expressing it. What about the parts of our lives that we never thought needed our love? If we gain a better understanding of this tricky concept, we'll be able to spread love in everything we do, from our homes to our workplaces.

The philosophical foundation of love is worth a quick look. The Greeks rocked the house with their depiction of seven types of love, but you may find yourself struggling with pronunciation. We certainly did. Here's how the Greeks viewed love in today's lingo (see table 1):

Storge. Ever try to describe the love feeling you have for your offspring, sometimes known as children, and directly applicable except during the teenage years? This would also apply to parents and to well-behaved brothers and sisters. This love is problematic to describe, but we use it often, mostly on Mother's Day or Father's Day. We love our family regardless of their personality or political leanings (except during the holidays when forced to sit through a dinner of turkey or ham). This is what *storge* (pronounced "store-jay") describes. It is not physical or sexual, but rather family-like, or familiar. It stems from some level of dependency, especially early on (child to parent) and later on (parent to child).

Philia. Has anyone ever told you that you should date your best friend or that long-lasting relationships start with friendship? This friendship love is called philia, and it is all about affection and not romance. You don't have to be physically or sexually attracted to feel philia. Philia, the love you have for another, is more about being able to trust the person, see the good in the person, and be able to depend on the person. So, as far as the phrase "Let's just be friends," well, maybe that ain't so bad? Nah, it's pretty bad. Sorry. The good news is that this friendship love is usually shared between equals, and at some point in this love relationship each person grows with the other because of mutual respect, admiration, and trust.

Eros. Eros is the love we most often think of when we say love. Yes, this is what we refer to when we say we are madly in love, or we fell in love, or we found the one. And no thanks to movies that often depict this love in inaccessible ways by creating scenarios that make us feel a little inadequate when searching for the love of our life! Eros is the love that describes a physical, sexual, heart-stopping love we feel for another person, and not always in a dimly lit room after many drinks. This love is described as romantic, as passionate, and sometimes as madness (which happens to be the name of our sailboat). Some attest that eros doesn't last past the honeymoon stage, but others say it can last a lifetime. So, the next time you encounter someone for whom you feel this pull, tug, or connection and you just can't stop thinking about them, remember it is love, eros love.

Table 1. Greek Love at a Glance

Storge	"I love ya like a sister."
Philia	"I value our friendship so very much."
Eros	"I can't think of anyone but you."
Pragma	"Yeah, we've been together forever. So there's that!"
Agape	"No matter what, I'll always love you."
Ludus	"Wow, you're hot!"
Philautia	"I'm okay."

Pragma. This is a love that evolves over time, between two people who basically decided to make it work, regardless of what might be missing with respect to passion or attraction. It is often found between people who have been together for so long, they have learned how to compromise for the good of the partnership. So that silence you hear at Grandma and Grandpa's house may simply be pragma love. It may have started with eros, but over time the mutual goals became more important than individual goals or even individual happiness. In the best of cases, it may be philia-like if the couple remain friends. However, pragma in its purest form is much more identifiable in situations where a couple stays together out of a contractual sense of obligation. Sadly, this love is more common than one might think.

Agape. Think Mother Teresa. This unconditional, all-giving love is not often experienced or seen. Few people can truly exhibit this love over a long period of time because it is the kind of love that requires a human being to give at an almost-superhuman level. Sometimes described as spiritual and otherworldly, agape is exhibited by people who would suffer in order to ensure the happiness of others. This is more than simply holding the door open for someone who needs help or dropping a few dollars in someone's violin case, hat, or cup. It has no conditions and serves only the best interest of others. It has been described as altruism; however, altruism also comes with phys-

Did you know that capuchin monkeys and chimpanzees express love by showing that they prefer the greater-good approach and not a selfish approach? In experiments, the capuchin and the chimpanzee consistently exhibit this altruistic behavior. When given a choice between different-colored tokens, where one color rewards only the self and the other color rewards both the self and the other monkey, the capuchin and the chimpanzee both consistently choose the color that rewards both.

iological benefits. Consider agape as a love that is felt for others, and for all others, at one's own expense.

Ludus. Think back to the days when you and your friends would go out and hit a bar. If you still do this, we're up for hearing the stories! You do a little people watching. And then you see it, someone scoping the scene and catching the eye of another at the far end of the room. The playful dance ensues: eye contact, sauntering, smiling from ear to ear, turning on the charm, and being coy. Both parties know that this may or may not lead to anything serious, but who knows? The folks you're observing don't know each other, so this can't be eros love. Nonetheless, there is something there, a level of infatuation and discovery, and a little wooing. You are witnessing *ludus* love, or playful love. This could lead to more, but at that moment there are no commitments, just this desire to seduce or be seduced by this person. Ludus could potentially turn into the "friends with benefits" scenario, and we'll leave it at that!

Philautia. *Philautia* is the love that matters most, the love for self. Without this love, you cannot truly love another. We are not talking about narcissism or self-centeredness or even self-confidence. Philautia is about being able to love yourself enough to forgive yourself, nurture yourself, be kind to yourself, and take care of yourself. This includes self-esteem and a sense of self-worth. We have all heard the saying "You can't take care of someone you love if you don't take care of yourself." Even the airlines ask you to put on your own oxygen mask before attending to your child. Being able to recognize your worth and value, respecting yourself, and exhibiting self-compassion are paramount to being able to lead and love those you lead. This kind of love alleviates the need to be recognized by others, or lauded by your own leadership, or being the star of the show. When you feel this kind of love, you are not seeking validation or recognition externally because you already know and love yourself with all of your gifts, flaws, strengths, and weaknesses. You recognize, accept, and love the real you.

Importantly, and above all of the other types of love mentioned previously, philautia is crucial for one's ability to lead others. When you possess this authentic, humble self-love, you are able to open yourself up to growth and development. You love yourself. You accept who you are. You are not afraid of failure and are open to taking risks. This includes both personal or professional relationships. Philautia opens up the possibility of growing, stretching, and learning about yourself and those around you. A setback does not destroy someone strong in philautia. Failure doesn't lessen their self-value or give way to blame and ridicule. Letdowns result in forgiving of self and others.

Since the Greeks created their conceptions of love, the world saw love manifest itself in numerous ways over time. Love was the focus of many musicals and plays through the Middle Ages and the Renaissance, and into the modern age. Movies, television shows, and novels commonly tell the story of love. And as stories were told, images of love emerged.

He whom love touches not walks in darkness. —Plato

Symbols of love abound. One might ask, why is this important? They are there for a reason—to remind us of love. These symbols remind us that love exists, that we need love in our lives, and that we feel love. And for the record, this is not lost on people in the

Figure 1. Symbols of love

workplace. Think about it—do we ignore and not even think about love while at work? We'll get to that.

So what about these symbols, and where are they? Figure 1 provides a quick glance at what many of these may look like. No one could stroll through the Greek conceptions of love without mentioning Cupid—a messy amalgamation of Greek and Roman mythology. He was known to the Greeks as Eros and to the Romans as Cupid, an infant child (with muscles?) wielding a bow and a quiver laden with golden arrows and targeting unsuspecting souls with affection, love, and attraction. Why a baby was ever allowed to play with a bow and arrows is beyond our comprehension, but this did predate child labor laws and modern social services organizations.

But let's give Cupid a break. The dude was an early symbol of love among the masses and continues to dominate the "Oh, that reminds me of love" landscape. So, he has that going for him. And symbols matter. They allow free association, often immediate, with emotions and feelings. Their importance can't be denied. The "right" logo on a handbag, a polo shirt, or the hood of a car sends an instant message to the recipient. No extraneous talk necessary!

Many symbols have competed for top billing with Cupid. First on the list is the heart, the origin of which is not, despite how much we'd like it to be, from the box of sweetheart candies originally produced by Necco. These Valentine's Day faves had subtle messages imprinted on the candy and probably contributed more to the spread of the common cold than sneezing in a subway or sharing a tissue with a stranger.

Nope. The origin of the heart is far more muddled, everything from a cooking herb to a part of the human anatomy. The herb argument stems from a large species of fennel called silphium found on the North African coastline, shaped much like a heart. It served the Greeks and Romans in a range of ways, including as birth control, a cooking herb, and medicine. It must have worked because it was extinct by the first century AD. Other than the fennel theory, the heart-shaped symbol, depending on whom you talk to, may have originated from European playing cards, an ivy leaf, religion, or a water lily. Artists in the Middle Ages are sometimes given credit for the heart, as they produced anatomical drawings as part of the study of medicine. Other symbols of love exist as well, and the variety may astound you.

Apples—yes, the ones you probably picked up at the grocery store a few days ago—are associated with love. So is the apple blossom as a sign of ecstasy, abundance, fertility, adoration, or union. This reference is seen in China, where the blossom is linked to adulation, and appears a great deal in Greek mythology, where apples were presented as gifts at weddings or for the sole purpose of courting a goddess.

Another symbol of love, and often used for wooing, is roses. Ah, yes, the dozen red for Valentine's Day or to say "I'm sorry." Usually it works, and maybe that is because the rose still symbolizes not only love but devotion, honor, beauty, wisdom, and the idea of forever. In Greek mythology, Aphrodite, the goddess of love, is seen wearing roses, sometimes from head to toe, probably because it was from her lover Adonis's blood that the rose first emerged, symbolizing his eternal love for her. Speaking of blood, the red tulip symbolizes what some call perfect love. The short bummer story is that a prince fell in love, and when his lover was killed, he committed suicide. From every spot where his blood droplets touched, a red tulip bloomed.

Jewelry plays a role in the symbolic representation of love as well, sort of. The Celtic love knot is found in various designs that are often used in rings and necklaces. With no beginning or end, representing eternity, this design signifies never-ending love. The Claddagh ring symbolizes a legend about a fisherman who was separated from his love and was forced to work as a slave in Africa. This story inspired the creation of the Claddagh ring, depicting a heart with a crown being held up by two hands. We see these symbols in necklaces too, such as the menat symbol, from ancient Egypt. It was fashioned as a necklace made of many beads in a crescent shape in front with a counterweight at the back. This necklace was believed to bring about potency, fertility, joy, and good luck.

Let's not forgot our flying friends like the ladybug, who may or may not be a lady. The ladybug is purported to be an indication of good luck, and in the Asian culture it also represents love. The story is that if you capture a ladybug and release it, it will find your true love and drop a hint by saying your name, and your newly found love will somehow search you out on the internet (this is true, except for the internet part). The best part is that you can pretty much guess when you should be all dressed up and waiting because the number of spots on the ladybug's back will tell you how many months it will take for that love to find you. Maybe this was the precursor to today's dating websites?

Other symbols that fly are evident in some of our more common birds. A careful observation of two swans facing each other reveals the obvious heart shape formed by their necks and heads. And who hasn't been to a wedding where a basket of doves are released, hopefully without incident? Doves are liberated at weddings because it is believed that doves will seek out and find their soulmates on Valentine's Day, the national day of love. Lovebirds are also a symbol of love because of their affectionate personalities; they will sit side by side, cozying up and cooing with their partner for hours, rarely being apart. Some suggest that lovebirds are unable to survive without their mate, so maybe the relationship is more pragma, but for the purposes of this book, we'll stick with the love angle.

Lastly, we would be remiss if we didn't give Valentine's Day a shout-out as a love symbol. On February 14 each year, untold numbers of people flock to the store to purchase heart-shaped knick-knacks, candies, and chocolates. Millions more buy roses or other symbols of love. Not many buy apples, and frankly, that would be received well by only the most astute observer of love. Nonetheless, on February 14 we all get to witness the panicked American wandering the aisle of the neighborhood grocery store, having completely forgotten what day it was and seeking to purchase a suitable symbolic gift. Is nothing on sale?

What is so strange is that the origin of Valentine's Day is fraught with some pretty grisly stuff. It was named after the Roman priest born in AD 226 who was reported to have encouraged marriage among the populace and was imprisoned by Emperor Claudius II. During his imprisonment he became close (more philia than eros) to Julia, the daughter of one of the jailers, Asterius. He was sentenced to die in a most gruesome fashion. Just prior to his death, he sent a kind note to Julia—the first Valentine's Day card. He signed it, "From your Valentine." The rest is history.

Enough about the types of love and the symbols that we see to remind us of love. Let's get to the topic of love. What is it? Selflessness? Affection? Warmth? Compassion? Attraction? We learned a little in our search for love from Greek philosophers, studly infants, kitchen herbs, doves, and an imprisoned priest. But we still fall short. Fast-forward to pop culture, and there's no shortage of attempts to capture what love is, ranging from Aretha to Beyoncé to Manilow. Love remains a topic of great interest in the worlds of philosophy, advertising, poetry, and science. People with lots of degrees do their best to capture what love is, and isn't, and how it impacts us. Love appears in various forms, but the fact is, love transcends all of our attempts to define it.

We know that acts of love and compassion predate our conscious memories. Researchers have shown, for example, that eighteen-month-old children will seek to comfort another if they sense sadness. This is before their perception of exchange develops, so there's nothing in it for them that they know of. Very young children don't make the assessment that if they show compassion, they will get something in return. This tells us that love is biological and part of the human makeup.

In a fascinating ongoing study—since 1938, to be precise—scientists at Harvard recruited 268 sophomores to attempt to assess the secret to a happy and healthy life. As of 2017, 19 of the original 238 were still alive, and the data collected by what is referred to as the Harvard Study of Adult Development revealed the role that love and relationships play as we age. Contrary to popular belief, neither IQ nor socioeconomic circumstances had the same level of impact. Individuals with loving parents and with good relationships with sisters and brothers were happier and more successful than others.

Let's think of love as an intensely intimate state of being, one where we connect at a personal level with those we care about—and yes, even those we lead. It exudes from deep within our soul, heart, mind, and body. Love is humanity embodied. It's multifaceted and beautiful, even if we can't put it into words. It's more than a feeling, an emotion, or a scripted action—the latter of which is where leaders consistently fall short (more on that later). Charles Darwin once suggested that love was the distinctive human characteristic that allowed our species to thrive (Loye 2000). The resulting social network that humans build allows for the nurturing and care required for a species to survive. Makes sense. One thing we know for sure is that love has a biological and physiological impact on all of us.

Did you know that elephants are very touchy-feely animals when they love? Elephants rub each other with their trunks to show care for each other, and when a male and female are in love, they will intertwine their trunks to show that they are together and can be seen constantly touching each other, whether it be the tail, the ears, the trunk, or a simple body-to-body touch while standing close by. Elephants exhibit mourning rituals for those they have loved and lost, whether they be other elephants or humans. The ritual with other elephants is elaborate, where they stay by the body and cover it with foliage, in a way burying the body. They sit by the body for a week or more and even visit the "grave site" year after year. There is even a story of a longtime elephant conservationist who worked at the Thula Thula Reserve, who passed away in his home one and a half years after retiring. Somehow the elephants knew, and two herds of elephants on the reserve whom he had cared for walked for twelve hours to the caretaker's home and held vigil for two days, mourning the loss of their loved one.

What Happens When We Love and When We Don't

That feeling we get when we love, or when we're loved, is like no other. Some may describe it as a warm, cozy feeling. Others claim it feels like nausea. It's actually both. And when love is absent in our lives, we experience feelings as well: emptiness, loneliness, even illness. Love has a way about it, physiologically and psychologically.

Consider the body's reaction to love the equivalent of a chemistry experiment gone mad. Having a fundamental understanding of the brain's role in love is important for two reasons: it's cool and it makes you sound smart at parties. *I'm thinkin' there's a little dopamine activity happening over there in the corner!* All kidding aside, the complexity of the human physiological reaction to love is remarkably convoluted and in some aspects unknown. Scientists suspect that the neural activity related to love occurs in the hippocampus, the medial insula, the ventral tegmental area, the caudate nucleus, and the anterior cingulate cortex, among other Latin-sounding parts of our brain that we can't spell. So, let's keep this simple. A foundational overview is definitely worth the effort. Why in the world would anyone want to lead with love if they didn't understand what love does to us physiologically? We want to help you understand the *why* behind love in the workplace before the *how*.

Let's start with dopamine, that pesky little neurotransmitter sending signals all over the place, like the internet signal we wish we had. When dopamine is front and center, we have a robust desire to bond with others and feel that lighter-than-air feeling. Toss in some norepinephrine to enhance alertness and a corresponding decrease in serotonin, and before you know it, we are focusing on the object of our love to the point that we may do some off-the-wall things, like sending heart emojis, or apples, every five minutes. We're still struggling with that apple thing.

Other neurochemicals play the love game as well. Oxytocin levels increase. Sounds familiar, right? Oxytocin has become a popular topic in leadership literature over the years. It enhances the feeling of bonding and helps build trust and empathy. To be fair, oxytocin has another face, and not a nice one. In some cases, it can lead one to be jealous or suspicious. Additionally, levels of the hormone vasopressin rise, contributing to the bonding feeling. And if you feel a little stressed, it's because the level of the hormone cortisol increases, at least initially.

One of the more intriguing outcomes of the love dynamic is limbic resonance, which would be a great name for a band! Researchers have made a compelling argument that the limbic system, the part of the brain that controls such things as behavior, motivation, memory, and emotions, plays a significant part in the way human beings bond with one another. In their groundbreaking work, psychiatrists Thomas Lewis, Fari Amini, and Richard Lannon discovered that our nervous systems are not self-contained; rather, they harmonize with others around us (Lewis et al. 2000). The idea, without using really big words, is that our nervous systems communicate with each other in a sort of neurological dance. We feel it when we're in the presence of someone we connect with. It's a positive vibe. And it's pretty cool.

Psychologically, love feels, well, like love. And not just romantic love. Living a life with supportive, caring relationships can help us live longer and stay healthier. We are less self-conscious and enjoy higher levels of self-esteem. Love can also boost our immune systems and combat depression. We're happier. And after that initial blast of cortisol returns to normal, we reach a blissful balance, a flow where we are more content with life.

The absence of love in our life is a sad state of affairs. When we do not love, or we are unloved, the impact on our being can be extreme. Declining self-esteem, depression, and emotional disconnection can occur. Even in the earliest stages of our lives, babies who do not experience holding and cuddling may show developmental delays or illness. One study found that infants who suffered from a lack of suitable physical and emotional attention registered different levels of vasopressin and oxytocin in their systems, even after having spent three years in a family setting (Fries et al. 2005). Recall that these two hormones are critical in later life for bonding and connection with other humans.

Social isolation not only contributes to a lack of love in our communities but also has been shown to directly contribute to higher mortality rates. In fact, isolation and loneliness is especially troublesome when seeking love in our lives. A groundbreaking 2015 meta-analysis by Julianne Holt-Lunstad and a team of neuroscientists and psychologists at Brigham Young University revealed that social isolation increased the chances of early death by 29 percent, and loneliness increased the rate of mortality by 26 percent—no matter the subject's age, gender, location, or culture (Holt-Lunstad et al. 2015). Cigna's U.S. Loneliness Index found that in 2020, 61 percent of Americans reported being lonely (Cigna 2020).

It seems logical, doesn't it? We depend on one another. We need one another. We need to love one another. And since we know that research connects love, attachment, and social bonding to the human limbic system, we know this is driven from deep within ourselves. But it transcends self. We are interconnected with those with whom we come in contact, those we are most close to, and those we lead. We have a biological imperative for love and all the wonderful accouterments—kindness, gratitude, empathy. Dopamine, serotonin, and oxytocin all dance a beautiful jig in making this happen. Love matters, or it should. And if it matters, what's wrong with love in leadership?

Where there is love, there is life. —Mahatma Gandhi

When Love Is Missing in Leadership

By this time, we're thinking that we have you on the hook for learning a few new Greek words and recognizing the importance of love. And when it comes to a dear friend, a puppy, a partner, or a relative, who's to disagree, right? So why not in the workplace? Why not as the foundation of our leadership practice?

We can hear the doubters now.

Zina and Patrick, it's not professional.

Zina and Patrick, we have to have boundaries in the workplace.

Zina and Patrick, I run a tight ship.

The words *love* and *leadership* are not often coupled together. Leadership author and advisor Mike Myatt said it well:

> While love and leadership are certainly two words you don't often hear in the same sentence, I can assure you that rarely does great leadership exist without love being present and practiced. In fact, if you examine failed leaders as a class, you'll find that a lack of love, misplaced love, or misguided love were a contributing cause of said failures, if not the root cause (Myatt 2012).

God bless ya, Mike.

Sadly, too many managers have historically considered expressions of love as inappropriate and crossing the line. Give us a break!

Did you know that our dogs do love us back? A Japanese study examined the oxytocin levels in humans and in dogs after they spent time playing with each other and looking into each other's eyes. After thirty minutes of play time, the oxytocin levels in humans increased by 300 percent. In dogs, the oxytocin levels increased by 57.2 percent after just ten minutes and 130 percent after thirty minutes. If you look your dog in the eyes, the dog will look back into your eyes, and yup, you got it, the love hormone increases on both sides. Cats in the same study exhibited a 12 percent increase in oxytocin levels after spending ten minutes with their owner. In another study, and coming to the felines' defense, cats do seem to be happier interacting with their owners as opposed to eating.

The line? What line? The human line? There seems to be an inherent tension for some when discussing the ultimate soft skill and coupling it with our role as leaders. There's a fear of the softness, the unexplained, and the complex. And that's precisely what love requires: a comfort with the unknown. We're dealing with human hearts and souls here. It's not part of a manual, and there is no certification at the end of the tunnel. It's unpredictable raw human emotion full of tears, joy, and fright. Engaging love is novel, and scary, so many leaders fear the presence.

Contrast this with the comfort level that many find with our habitual patterns of leading. Look closely. One of the most common approaches is the documented checklists of what we should be doing, or what someone with a lot of TED Talks told us we should be doing. To wit: The leader heads to work. Before exiting the subway or getting out of his car, he refers to his "I'm a Whatever Leader" pocket guide, which takes him step-by-step through the process that will guarantee leadership infamy and ultimate success. Our leader steps out onto a busy street, rehearsing just what to do in his mind.

He's got this! It's a simple acronym like ILEADWELL or DOGFOOD or something catchy. The leader arrives at the office and the process begins. He stops at each office, every cubicle, with a forced "Good morning!" Check. "How are the kids?" Check. "How was your weekend?" Check. This is the leadership equivalent of the golf-clap, the polite approval of sinking a two-foot putt. It's nothing more than the obligatory. It stems from our comfort with predictable processes, not from real human connection.

This contentment with the predictable originates from the way we think. We ask that you reread those last two sentences again. We'll wait . . .

Yes, this takes us back to the brain! Consider the process by which the brain works. When we have a thought, neurons fire and connect along a neural pathway. Have those thoughts more often and we form a neural pathway. This pathway becomes our default way of thinking. It's our go-to. From a psychological and evolutionary perspective, this makes sense. We have a characteristic human need for steadiness and predictability. We like the consistent. We need to know our place in the world, and if we're a teenager, that very world revolves around us—sorry, couldn't resist. But these thinking patterns serve another very important purpose. They allow us to maintain a stable sense of self, and this matters for our self-esteem and perception of self-worth.

Professionally, this type of patterned thought can be of great benefit to us. We master the technical thinking and skills necessary to hold a job or get a promotion. It's far simpler to assess employee performance and compare staff skills. Personnel decisions are marvelously more understandable because we reduce our leadership responsibilities to solely measuring performance goals. We compare the completion of a project or the attainment of a certification across those we lead, and decision made! No love needed! This thinking can also be very helpful for quick problem-solving and reactions to emergencies. In these situations, our brain quickly finds that pre-established path, and bingo! Problem solved. Danger avoided.

So this is good, right? Not so fast. Yes, it helps us maintain a secure sense of who we are. Yes, it solidifies our perception and proficiency with the skills we bring to the table. But that's it. The familiar sights, sounds, and experiences that envelop the predictable thought process may make us content, but they don't allow us to stretch our minds or face instability. By centering ourselves on only what we're most content with, and seeing only what is visibly measurable, we are blind to growth and bound to the status quo (or, as one of our authors refers to it, the "standard quo," which, when you think about it, is actually correct as well!).

And this is precisely how love fails to make it into our leadership. We depend on established business processes, practice our deep-voice presentation style, ensure that we are seen in all the right places and have all the right books on our table. It's easy. It's process. It's predictable. And it's not love.

Our teams notice. Why? Because that limbic resonance isn't there. Those we lead don't feel it. They don't *feel* it. People want emotion in their lives, and that includes the good and the bad. Happiness, disappointment, sadness, love. It enriches us. Researchers have uncovered evidence of strong links between emotions in the workplace and employee wellness and engagement. And these effects impact the bottom line. When positive emotional support and a fabric of caring are not present, mission accomplishment suffers. Sadly, our organizations are underperforming due to a lack of love on the part of our leaders.

Fiona Beddoes-Jones, PhD, founder and CEO of the Cognitive Fitness Consultancy in Grantham, England, presents a harsh reality. She found a longing for connection and love in her research on workplaces. Her research found that 65 percent of respondents felt there was a lack of love in organizations (Beddoes-Jones 2017).

A few other significant findings from her work:

- Ninety-six percent said they would work harder in an organization where they felt genuinely cared for.

- Seventy percent believed that their general well-being at work would be enhanced if their organizational culture had more love.
- Eighty-three percent proposed that leaders and managers should be educated on how to love their staff.

Love. Not strategic planning. Not re-skilling. Not design thinking. Love. Beddoes-Jones describes this not as romantic love (eros) but rather as compassion, caring, and kindness. Is that so hard? And it's not as though our workforce doesn't deserve it. Now, more than ever, we are struggling with fear, anxiety, and loneliness. We are a nation in need. And we are in need of love in every part of our life.

OK, we know that we sound direct here, and nothing personal, but this falls squarely in the lap of leaders. Leaders are to blame. Sometimes we simply fail to see the value of love because we do not consider it a necessary part of organizational productivity, metrics, and structure. If it's not on the organizational chart, it must not matter. If it's not embedded in our annual 342-page strategic plan, in which we invest countless resources and which *no one ever reads,* it must be unimportant. Love gets left out.

We have all sorts of excuses for our oversight, some rather adorable. Leaders love to depend on catchphrases that they pull from some dank place and hang their very reputations on. You may hear, "It's the mission that matters." OK, got it. And I recall seeing the mission statement in the elevator. So, yeah, mission matters. At what cost? Or the next-of-kin phrasing "Mission first, people always!" Gotcha. So, we're thinking we've covered all the bases with that one, huh? People are always there to perform the mission? Or are people always people? We're lost on this one.

Some leaders are especially adept at avoiding the whole love-in-my-leadership debate. They all bring their own combination of charm, frustration, and silliness. But the sad fact is that we all fall in here somewhere, and it impacts our ability to love and lead. Here are a few examples:

The "I Got This" leader. Ah, the comfort we all must feel when this pronouncement is made. Things are going to be just fine because this leader has seen it all before. No questions necessary. Her wisdom and expertise know no bounds, and she is certain that her past experiences and vast knowledge will guarantee future success. We'll revisit this leader a little later.

The "Catchphrase" leader. Imagine a conversation in which the leader uses every book title (except ours, of course), every acronym, and the latest biz lingo, all in one sentence. It happens! Too much surface here and not any depth. You can often find this leader in bookstores memorizing book titles.

The "Selfie" leader. This leadership type is a little scary because it borders on narcissism. In its worst form, this refers to leaders known for their grandiose self-image and lack of concern for others. They may be found bending over streams gazing at themselves. This type can also be driven by a serious lack of self-worth, with a soul that is searching for validation or approval from others.

The "Call Me by My Title" leader. Enough already. This is one of our biggest pet peeves. "Uh, call him Professor Malone, please! And that would be Dr. Sutch!" Love knows no titles. And hanging our importance or stature on the title in front of our name serves no purpose other than to inflate our ego. Not terribly conducive to love.

The "Show Me the Metrics" leader. Can we please not bow at the altar of metrics for just a few minutes? Measuring the most important things in life is much more complex than trending data. Connection, trust, feeling, and love all matter more. They set the stage for everything that's measurable.

The "I Don't Even Like Myself" leader. By far the saddest of all, but this type does exist. Activist and author Parker Palmer once suggested that there is nothing inherently wrong with self-care. He considered it stewardship of the most valuable thing we possess, ourselves. The ancient Greeks knew this. Philautia is the love that matters most.

Let's not be too hard on ourselves. We all fall in here somewhere. We are imperfect humans and really imperfect leaders. But the answer is right there in front of us, and it is an urge we feel from infancy. Love is more than just OK. It is an absolute imperative if we are to be the leaders we want to be, to be the people we want to be. The word *love* has to become the core of who we are as a person before we can even imagine being the leader we want to be—even if we don't know it.

So, Try This

- Think about the Greek philosophies of love. Which resonates with you the most?
- Try counting the number of times you use the word *love* in your life and how you use it.
- Have you ever written a leadership philosophy for yourself? If you have, look back and see if you use the word *love* anywhere. Don't cheat, we'll be watching.

How You Know You Are Letting Go and Getting Real

- How do *you* feel? Are you noticing a bit more joy in your own heart? Less stress? Are you breathing deeper? Are you smiling more often?
- How do your team members interact? Are your team members celebrating each other's successes and their personal and workplace milestones?
- How do your team members interact with you? Do you know more about each of your team members? Does giving feedback and receiving feedback feel easier?

Love recognizes no barriers. It jumps hurdles, leaps fences, penetrates walls to arrive at its destination, full of hope. —Maya Angelou

And Finally

When we understand what love truly is and the role it plays in our lives, we come to a sad conclusion: love is missing. We work with senior leaders across the country, and it never ceases to amaze us how often we underestimate the need for love, caring, empathy. Yes, they seek best practices. Yes, they seek the latest research. Yes, they seek strategic focuses on how to do design thinking and the like. But what they eventually acknowledge is their need for connection.

Love matters. It matters because with all that we have learned with respect to phenomenal leadership approaches, models, and philosophies, we still fail. Organizations still have toxic work environments, and pompous leaders unintentionally or even intentionally insult those they lead. The workforce is anxiety-ridden, lonely, and frightened. The latest leadership reports published by organizations that we all know the names of never mention the word *love*. Anywhere. When we fail to recognize the human need and capacity to love, we fail as leaders. Love is the crucial component in our lives, and our very survival depends upon its presence. In a perfect world, love abounds. Why not in the world of leadership?

CHAPTER 2

LEADERS WHO LOVE

It's actually kind of interesting. When we type into a search engine various combinations of "love," "love workplace," "love leadership," and the like, we get a lot of hits—but not the ones we were hoping for. What we see are lots of articles on love in the workplace. Like, romance love. Like, who's-the-new-data-analyst-and-do-you-think-there's-a-dinner-date-on-the-horizon love in the workplace. Ah, the salacious details of office romance. Sorry, we'll admit that the topic would be a fun one to explore, but not in this book! When we say leaders who love, you know what we mean—and what we don't. Think of it as a companion-like love—a love entailing connection and warmth. Yep, we'll go with that!

Love rightly exists in the finest leaders, and it is a beautiful thing to behold. Leaders who love create environments of compassion and caring. Why? Because they have compassion, and they care! And not the kind of artificial compassion and care marked by the scheduled all-hands meeting where the leader brings the coffee and doughnuts, and staff members get to ask obligatory questions. We're talking real love here, the kind that comes from the heart and radiates vulnerability and kindness. It is the kind of love that transforms organizations and becomes legendary. It's real.

An argument could be made that leaders who love have some sort of organizational advantage that allows them to have a reputation for love, but this would be a faulty assumption. There are of course the big companies we all know about, and their leadership gets lots of credit for their approach to love. The Container Store, with their "We Love Our Employees Day," engages in some endearing and wacky activities each year to show love to their team. PepsiCo, Zappos, and Southwest Airlines all make use of the words *love* and *caring* in their organizational principles. Southwest Airlines even has a heart as their logo, and their flight attendants are really funny.

The truth is, there is no one-size-fits-all type of organization for loving leaders. Most come from organizations we have never heard of. They hail from small, midsize, and large companies. They face financial hardships, difficult personnel decisions, and technology barriers. They work in competitive environments with dwindling resources and the ever-present challenge of recruiting top talent. In short, they come from everywhere. And they love.

The leaders we admire the most are not simply following a protocol, implementing the latest trendy strategy, or using some established format or silly gimmick to create a culture. They don't depend on the most popular leadership gurus to guide them. Rather, they have tapped into their own hearts, have recognized what is most important to themselves as a human being, and exude it into the universe around them. They know what they're doing. Let's have a look at a couple of them.

Our Love Heroes

Love Hero #1

Imagine being in a workplace where you hear words like these spoken by your colleagues: "We all gelled right away" and "It was just real chill, like a family atmosphere, just genuine love." When asked what made the environment so great, the response was, "We'd have these long conversations about . . . anything." Or, "It was pretty cool to see how we would all get super-focused and locked in. It was really fun with this group. We got so close and had each other's backs. Everybody was genuinely happy for each other and having so much fun." And this: "It was incredible. I'll never forget how fun that time was." And still another noted, "We knew we could do it if we stuck together and didn't listen to any of the outside stuff. And we came out on top."

And what about a team lead who says, "About the legacy of this team, it's really tough for me not to get emotional. They had all of those things: passion, great skill, incredible leadership, unselfishness, a love for one another, and on and on." Uh, like wow. We want some of that.

Reread these statements and imagine who this leader may have been. Ideas?

While you're thinking, ponder this: Is this how you would describe your team? Sometimes as leaders we have to face the music—either our teams are like this one, or not. Do our teams have the passion, the fun, the commitment, and the care for one another? What made this team come together, love one another, and have fun?

These quotes came from Dawn Staley's team members. You may or may not have heard of Dawn. She is not a CEO of a famous company. She doesn't produce leadership YouTube videos. She doesn't teach leadership development classes. She isn't the author of the latest best-selling leadership book. She is a basketball coach, and a pretty doggone good one. Our bet is, she's improved the lives of more people than most we know. As the coach of the women's basketball teams at Temple University and the University of South Carolina, she did just that. And guess what? She took her teams to the top.

Dawn is a former Women's National Basketball Association star. She played professionally in the American Basketball League and the Women's National Basketball Association (WNBA), where she was voted in as one of the top fifteen players in WNBA history and inducted into the Women's Basketball Hall of Fame in 2012. Prior to her professional basketball success, she was a player who was a three-time Olympic gold medalist, played for the University of

Virginia, and was a gold medal winner at the 1996 Summer Olympics. Talent? We think so!

She didn't really want to coach, but she still accepted the head coach role at the University of South Carolina in 2008 and brought her team to the number one ranking in the country, winning the Southeastern Conference (SEC) championships after only six seasons. We all know this is only because she was a tough, demanding, screaming, and scary coach who kept players on edge. Except we would be wrong. By her own words, Dawn wasn't focused on winning. She cared more about the players and their work-life balance than winning games, and it paid off. Her love-first approach yielded five SEC regular season championships, five SEC tournament championships, six Sweet 16s, two Final Fours, and South Carolina's first NCAA Women's Basketball National Championship. Her team was on its way to the 2020 Summer Olympics in Tokyo when COVID-19 hit and everything came to a halt.

The environment that Dawn cultivated was not only about the technical aspects of basketball but also about the broader cause. Her team members all had a 3.0 or better in the classroom, and they all contributed to the community in which they lived. Their community contributions were built around the idea of giving hope to others, sort of like what their coach did for them. Dawn had an extraordinary skill in bridging the dreams she envisioned for the team and using that as a platform for encouraging them to give hope to others.

Beyond the basketball court, Dawn established the Dawn Staley Foundation to offer at-risk children in Philadelphia skills they need to grow and become good, responsible citizens through after-school programs and mentoring. She also recognized early in her life how important sneakers were to children in low-income areas and made a commitment to help bring new pairs of shoes to the children in her community. The program, Innersoles, extended far beyond shoes. It focused on academics, attendance, behavior, and physical fitness.

During her induction into the Women's Basketball Hall of Fame in 2012 and the Naismith Memorial Basketball Hall of Fame in

2013, Dawn was quoted as saying that she knew she had made the right decision to coach when, as she stated, she cared more about the players than about winning the game. And this, our friends, is the biggest question leaders can ask themselves: Do you care more about your team members, or do you care more about yourself, your mission, and your accomplishments? It sounds harsh, and it may make you uncomfortable, but what do you care more about, self or others? Be honest.

She didn't really want to coach. Did we say that already? Maybe this sends a message.

Love Hero #2

Everyone goes to the grocery store. Well, we suppose some order their groceries online and have them delivered, but you get the idea. Let's be honest, grocery stores are pretty tame places by their nature. Everything is organized by type, size, and color. For those of us who like symmetry, it's heaven. And there's food, which means taco fixin's.

Even still, grocery markets, or chains of stores, can have their own drama, drama that is belied by the quiet aisles of goodies and polite clerks who know where to find the tahini. This love leader was a grocery guy, and he was so loved by his grocery market employees that when he was fired as CEO, six high-level managers resigned, and employees held rallies outside the grocery markets across Massachusetts and New Hampshire. While they didn't strike (they weren't part of a union), they participated in protests and demonstrations on their own time, including during their lunch and breaks.

Arthur T. Demoulas is a member of the family that started Market Basket. He joined the Board of Directors just out of high school, rose to president, and ultimately was revered by employees and community members as the one who fought the Board. His focus was on maintaining high wages and benefits for employees while still being able to provide the community with low prices.

In 2008, when Arthur became the president and CEO, he managed to expand the chain with sales growing from $3 billion to over $4 billion annually. Meanwhile, the size of the company doubled from 14,000 employees to 25,000 at a time when the grocery market was struggling and other grocery chains like Stop & Shop and Shaw's were closing many of their stores. It wasn't as if Arthur had not faced hardship. During the 2008 financial crisis, he forced the company to make up a $46 million loss so as not to negatively affect the employees' profit-sharing fund. He knew his business.

Arthur enjoyed a well-deserved reputation for caring more about his people than about profits. His Market Basket chain was known for its low prices and high-quality foods and became a community supplier especially for the elderly and those in low- and middle-income areas. He was also known for his ability to remember all of the employees' names (at all levels), birthdays, and even milestones in their lives. He attended many of their weddings and funerals, cared for them, asked about them, and knew them. Many described Arthur as a father figure, comparing him to George Bailey in *It's a Wonderful Life* for putting people before profit.

Then, due to a series of family disputes regarding the stores, he was fired. Family drama, what a shock!

When Arthur was let go, employees commenced the protesting. Unlike people at most demonstrations that would follow such an ousting, these employees were not demanding higher salaries, better benefits, or management changes. The employees at the family-owned Market Basket chain were paid just above minimum wage; they had great benefits, sick leave, and even a profit-sharing fund. They felt so well taken care of that they didn't need a union. Their commitment was to their CEO, whom they felt took great care of them. All they wanted was Arthur, nothing more. They wanted their kind-hearted leader back.

Giraffes played a role as well. During the demonstrations, employees held blown-up signs and photographs of their beloved CEO and carried stuffed-animal giraffes. You ask, "Why giraffes?" We asked the same thing. These employees were using giraffes to show the grocery market board and their community members that they were sticking their necks out for their CEO. They wanted him back.

The Board began firing employees for organizing rallies, but it backfired. Within twenty-four hours, an estimated five thousand people gathered outside the Market Basket in Tewksbury, Massachusetts. In his first statement to the public, Arthur called for the reinstatement of all those fired. Protests continued at all seventy-one of the stores, with managers and assistant managers preparing a petition stating that they would all resign if Arthur was not reinstated.

Demonstrations went on, with roughly three thousand employees and customers picketing at various store locations, warehouse workers and drivers refusing to make deliveries, and customers boycotting stores. This guy was loved! Governor Deval Patrick of Massachusetts and Governor Maggie Hassan of New Hampshire finally stepped in to help negotiate. Meanwhile, more than 160 mayors and legislators in Massachusetts and New Hampshire signed petitions agreeing to boycott Market Basket if Arthur was not reinstated.

Bipartisan? Amazing!

Arthur eventually returned, and the first thing he did was announce that all associates were welcome to come back to work and restore the company to normal. Employees were quoted as saying, “I feel like I won the lottery” and “I’m thrilled, this is epic.” Company bakers came in at midnight after Arthur made his statement and started baking cakes that read, “Welcome back Artie T: Market Basket Strong.”

If you can’t see the love here, put the book down!

What We Learn from Dawn and Arthur

Dawn and Arthur embodied love. How do we know? Look at those they touched, those who were willing to go an extra mile for them, support them, and love them. Both Dawn and Arthur excelled in creating environments where love ruled and where people mattered. Did they ever attend a leadership class or get a certification? Who cares? They didn't tout it if they did. What they did do was change lives.

Remember philia? These examples exhibit this kind of love, the love that is more about being able to trust the person, see the good in the person, and be able to depend on the person. As we defined earlier, this love is shared between equals, and at some point in this love relationship each person grows with the other because of mutual respect, admiration, and trust. Dawn and Arthur saw the good in their people, trusted them, depended on them, and also respected and admired them. They saw the human beings, not the players or key grocery employees—they saw and loved the people.

The other love that we see clearly is philautia. We identified this love as being crucial for one's ability to lead others. This is that authentic, humble self-love, where you are able to accept who you are and be open to taking risks in both personal and professional relationships. This self-love gave Dawn and Arthur the ability to keep growing and learning, not only about themselves, but also from those around them. Failures and setbacks didn't lessen their self-value or give way to blame, but rather strengthened their love for self and for others.

These leaders also understood the limits of a professional work relationship. Work affiliations are too often bound by a set of boxes and lines on organizational charts where protocol and practice is defined. Sometimes these norms exist through visible formal processes such as reports or weekly meetings. Sometimes they manifest themselves through more covert processes, like unspoken cultural rules. As much as your authors would advocate for joining hands and singing around the campfire, we have to admit that formality has some value, especially early on when people are navigating through multifaceted organizational structures and job responsibilities. There has to be some formality in order for organizations to function effectively—there, we said it!

But what happens? People get hired, and they learn the technical aspects of their jobs. They learn the requirements, what is expected, and what success looks like. We ease into a flow of performing the work we were hired to do. There is often a honeymoon period of sorts. "You are amazing! We're so glad we hired you!" Then things mature. If all we have between us is the work we do, we transcend into an exchange relationship. "Why didn't you finish that report? If you do this for me, I'll cover you." This is where relationships cease to be relationships between people. It is where work relationships begin to be contracts, sterile and void of passion. Nothing matters but the work being done.

This is precisely why these faux relationships have a breaking point, and it coincides strictly with the point where the contractual aspects of the relationship are established and a real relationship emerges. Or, it doesn't. Both Dawn and Arthur provide clear examples of relationships growing to a new plane. They bonded with those they led at a human level, not at a contractual one.

They accomplished this in unique ways. Dawn admitted that she cared more about the players than about winning. She instilled a sense of what was possible with her players and gave them a vision about what they could be. One can't do this following a matrix. It comes from the heart. She put her players first, focusing more on their well-being than on her own coaching résumé. If we can embrace her perspective on leadership, on how her coaching impacted her team's ability to succeed, we can realize the value of letting go and loving each one of our team members.

Dawn is just another human being, like you, and she doesn't have certifications or a license from a training program. She doesn't quote books or faddish approaches to leadership. She believes in and lives what she feels with her team. She exhibits her true love for the team and the game and seems to deeply understand that results are achieved when everyone is connected. When this happens, everyone trusts their own talents and the abilities of their team members.

Arthur's love approach was the direct cause of employees' holding rallies and customers' boycotting seventy-one grocery stores demanding his reinstatement. Employees on the picket lines would tell stories about how Arthur touched them personally. He checked on workers who were ill, asked and knew about their children and spouses, and offered comfort when needed. One employee shared that when his daughter was in a car accident, Arthur called him and asked about her. He then asked if the hospital was able to handle her injury and whether or not there was a need to move her to another facility.

Arthur fought for his employees first and foremost, and he treated all employees, at every level, like family. His employees didn't want to leave, because they felt loved and cared for. One manager noted that fifteen years later, he wouldn't work for anyone else. How many of those we lead would say that about us?

CHAPTER 3

THE LOVE BEHAVIORS

OK, so your authors had an argument over this chapter. Well, not really an argument, but a spirited discussion! The problem is, we agree on what you're about to read, but we also agree that it comes with risks. So maybe we didn't disagree at all. Here's what we mean.

There comes a time in every book when the reader is looking for the tips, the secrets, and the to-dos. Authors present a concept, define it, and then tell you how to get there. It's a simple and efficient methodology. It sells books, but it's not terribly effective. And that has been the shortfall of most leadership approaches, to our minds. Oh, the terminology is catchy to be sure. By suggesting that the following are the THREE BIG THINGS you need, or the FOUR BIG THINGS you need to do, this methodology lessens the importance of the main message—in this case, love.

One can't certify oneself in love. You can't check the box; get a red, yellow, or green belt; or read a few bullets, even the ones we present below, and consider yourself suitably prepared. Those are window dressing. They're a cheap and easy way to lay claim that one is now officially a certified loving leader. Spare us.

You can understand our concerns about offering, in this case, the THREE BIG THINGS we want you to think about, where love is concerned. When we make the argument below, we are not trying to convey the idea that these are the secret ingredients of love—they are not. You can't check a box and say, "Got it—next?" They are a conscious choice. They require deep introspection and intentional work over the course of our lives. They are principles you have to think about and try in all types of situations and environments. Remember, this is your choice to make. They are what we consider most important if and only if you can approach this with love first, genuinely, from the heart.

Your Love Choices

Self-Awareness

Parker Palmer, in his book *Let Your Life Speak*, poses a vexing question. He ponders how long it takes for a person to become the one that he or she has always been (Palmer 2000). How long does it take to become the person one has always been? Think about this for a minute. *No, seriously, one full minute.* Don't cheat. Go.

Welcome back. Palmer was onto something when he penned this haunting question. What he knew was that we often mask ourselves, and he suggests that we do so in faces that are not our own. But the primary reason why Palmer's challenge is such a good one is that he taps directly into the most fundamental component of emotional intelligence: self-awareness.

Emotional intelligence (EI) has been in the forefront of leadership development for the better part of fifty years. Its impact on leadership development has been significant. Far from the metric-worship of some approaches to leadership, emotional intelligence struck a personal note. It touched the heart and soul of leaders and forced them to become more aware of themselves and others. EI for leaders now matters more than ever because, as we know, leadership is not a framework. It's a connection between two human beings. It is a relationship.

Most manifestations of EI include at least four quadrants, though one may see them expanded to five or more. For our purposes, EI is best seen as a combination of the following:

- **Self-awareness:** Recognizing and understanding ourselves and our emotions
- **Self-management:** The ability to control our responses to our emotions
- **Social awareness:** Our prowess at spotting and assessing the emotions of others
- **Relationship management:** The outward manifestation of our application of EI in relationships with others

Exploring the above components of EI would take a book unto itself, but for our purposes, and as many researchers agree, the most significant part of EI is self-awareness. Practicing self-awareness allows us to search inside ourselves to discover and rediscover the people we truly are. It's an inward journey that frankly can be a little frightening. Seeing ourselves for who we are, not the way we wish to be seen, and not the way others see us, can bring a few surprises. Therein lies the beauty of self-awareness. As we explore ourselves, being open to seeing things we didn't expect, we hone who we are as leaders.

Leaders who exhibit strong self-awareness are comfortable in their own skin because they know who they are. They are in tune with their emotions and feelings—especially those inner signals that beleaguer them from time to time, such as feeling defensive when we're being offered feedback on our work. As we hear the words spoken, it's easy to feel that bit of discomfort in the abdomen. Perhaps we shift in our seat a little, adopting a more protective posture. Inside, our mind starts to race with responses to what we may perceive as an unfair attack. In the meantime, while our brain is forming the counterarguments necessary to respond, we miss the very chance to be open to learning. We miss an opportunity to grow and develop.

Now, let's take the above scenario and replay it using better self-awareness. As the comments come our way, we begin to feel all the emotions we described above. But because we've read this *amazing* book, highlighted it throughout, and written notes in the margins, we now know that the defensive retort that is forming is less than helpful. Bingo! We've just passed the self-awareness test! We were conscious of the sensations building up inside us. We acknowledged them. We know how they impact our performance. This is valuable beyond words. Simply seeing ourselves positions us to take action that would be more productive (by the way, that's the self-management piece of EI). Now, instead of arguing our point, we open our mind to what we may be missing in ourselves and what we can learn.

Achieving self-awareness is no easy task, to be sure. This is especially difficult when we try looking through the lens of who we are today. We can become so happy with our bad selves that we make the fundamental error of assuming that what got us here will get us there. Wrong. To be fair to our bad selves, we are at a disadvantage. We groom the people that we are, our pictures of ourselves through our prisms of education, family, tradition, faith, and society. It begins with our childhood. Some grow up in regimented, formal settings with schedules and deadlines, others in a more laid-back situation. Some families struggle with conflict, while others meet it head-on. Some are huggers, some are not. Some families use language like "I love you" often. Others avoid intimacy at all costs. As we mature, the things we believe, the suppositions we make, the values we hold, are continually sculpted through life experiences.

Rediscovering self, or new parts of self, can also feel like a transition as we move from our old selves to our new selves. Perhaps it's a first-gen college student who becomes the first degree holder in the family. It's not uncommon for these students to have a sense of confusion as to where they came from and who they are now as they continue their journey. The same thing can happen professionally. Let's say you begin your career working at a nonprofit that cares for the homeless. You have a deep passion for interacting directly with the needy and gain remarkable satisfaction from making a direct impact on their lives. Years down the line, you find yourself in a supervisor role, no longer interacting with those you serve, but rather with staff. The passion you feel for those you serve hasn't dissipated, though it may feel that way since you are in a different place in the organization.

In both of these cases, your core identity is still intact. Moving into different phases of life, or different phases of self, can make us question if we have forgotten the place we came from. We haven't. It remains. We've just chosen to continue growing. Think of it as a matryoshka doll—those little wooden dolls placed one inside another. Our smallest doll is our original self. We maintain the core of our original self. We don't shed it. We grow from it. And like a matryoshka doll, we get bigger and more beautiful as we do.

One more word on this. We so often congratulate ourselves for having a third-person perspective on a problem. We take a step back, or maybe to the side, and examine the situation from another angle. Then we tell everybody how wonderful we are because we took a third-person perspective on the problem. Yay us! A far more effective technique is to take a fourth-person perspective, but it requires self-awareness. In the fourth-person perspective, we take the time to observe ourselves looking at the problem. We examine ourselves first, embracing all of the biases we bring. This is self-awareness at its finest, and it's the first and most impactful step in getting to know ourselves. Think of it this way: If we don't know ourselves, how can we lead or love ourselves? And if we can't lead or love ourselves, how can we lead or love others? Start with self.

Vulnerability

Let's just put it out there now, and maybe again later, since we really want to make this point. There hasn't been a workplace survey in years where workers expressed their desire for their leadership to be more technically skilled than people skilled. And at the risk of frustrating our editor, we'd like to restate that: There hasn't been a workplace survey in years where workers expressed their desire for their leadership to be more technically skilled than people skilled. It's just the way it is. Yet leaders continue to make the same ill-conceived decision to lead from a technical mindset instead of a heart and soul mindset. Research tells us that our teams are looking for connection, engagement, and relatability. This does not happen without vulnerability.

Here's something interesting about the software we're using to write this book. Betcha didn't expect that sentence, did you? And no, you did not just stray off into another book completely unrelated to love and laughter. And no, this is not a misplaced sentence for another book we are writing. This will make sense, we promise. When we type in the word *vulnerability* and look for synonyms, here are the selections: *susceptibility*, *weakness*, *defenselessness*, *helplessness*, *openness*, *exposure*, *liability*. OMG, seriously? Among the top seven selections for a synonym for *vulnerability*, all of them but one (*openness*) denote weakness in some way. Sometimes the writing gods are on our side. Read on!

Vulnerability is not the first thing we typically associate with a strong leader. Historically, leaders have been portrayed as the loud, dominant, mysterious beings who have all of the answers and all of the vision. They're directive, to be sure. Bigger than life! It is comforting when you think about it, but it fails to allow for the engagement necessary to ensure that love is present in the workplace. Sadly, many of these boisterous leaders insist on being called by a title instead of the name they were given at birth. Maybe it's an ego thing or an image thing, but it is not an engagement thing. And it's certainly not a vulnerability thing.

Commonplace are the managers who fear that any display of empathy will render them as less than in charge, and far too often they view vulnerability as a lack of strength in the workplace. Fearful leaders fret over the risk of getting too close to a team member for fear of crossing some imaginary line of appropriateness. And as far as a show of emotion? No way. Tears are for the weak! Love is left at home. Leaders who eschew vulnerability will do nothing to negatively impact their stature and authority.

Fear of the *v*-word is not limited to personal interactions based on emotions like tenderness or forgiveness. Struggles with vulnerability may also find their origin in professional concerns. Leaders under pressure to meet their organization's mission may be unwilling to share information for fear of exposing what they do not know. Instead of reaching out for help, they hunker down in protective mode so as not to expose themselves. They may even blame external forces like "the bosses upstairs" or the company line as their foil. This easily devolves into the use of carefully crafted language to ensure that they say only the right thing.

To be fair, we are not neurologically wired to be vulnerable. The human brain loves those horizontal pathways of thought, consistent and predictable ways of thinking that give us great comfort. These allow us to make quick decisions and move forward. Definitely helpful during an emergency, since we default to them quickly. And this certainly fosters the image of the all-knowing leader. They are able to answer questions quickly and easily with little thought. No vulnerability required.

As we learned in our examination of self-awareness, some of our fears come from very early in life. Childhood experiences play an important role in our willingness to open ourselves up to others. Sadly, people who have felt distrust and hurt in their lives may be less willing to take a chance on exposing themselves to others. People who were raised in homes that were openly loving and affectionate are more adept at being willing to open themselves up. They have felt the risks of openness, but they've also experienced the rewards. The hard truth is that both apply to vulnerability.

Vulnerable leaders are willing to take risks. They recognize that vulnerability is about openness—a far cry from the depiction of susceptibility, weakness, defenselessness, helplessness, exposure, and liability suggested by a synonym search. Vulnerable leaders are straightforward and honest. Instead of parsing communication in a way to avoid bad news, they are open and candid with their observations and assessments. They're willing to admit that they don't know, and they ask questions of those who do. They are transparent when communicating with the teams they lead, creating an environment of shared information that allows for innovation, creativity, and open-ended questions. People are better informed and more willing to be vulnerable themselves, resulting in better decisions and more trust.

The practice of being vulnerable is a powerful way to model the behavior that we seek. Those in leadership positions often underestimate the degree to which their actions and words are scrutinized by others. By exhibiting vulnerability openly and honestly, leaders emerge as a focal point in their organization. People admire the ability of leaders to engage in an authentic way with those they lead. It may be in the form of a question, or in the practice of empathetic listening, but even the humblest attempt at letting one's guard down and relating to someone else can have a positive impact across an organization. Recognizing how we make people feel matters.

Finally, vulnerable leaders exhibit a fundamental leadership asset: they are themselves. They are original. Authentic. And they realize that being this way comes with measured risks. It's not perfect, but it's real, and real connects. It sends the message to those we lead that we're not above them, we are with them. They make mistakes; so do we. They don't know all of the answers, and neither do we. They have fears; so do we.

Look, we know there are risks here, and we're not suggesting being haphazard or foolish. Being vulnerable doesn't mean being an open book. It doesn't entail sharing all the sordid details about our lives. It also doesn't mean we don't hold ourselves and others accountable for performance. We do. It simply means we don't need to be the title we carry, just the person we are. It means we lead with our heart, and with love, and with caring. It means we need to be human first.

Kindness

At one point during the research for this book, we put the word *kindness* into Google Images. The results may surprise you. Kids. Lots of cute kids. While this is most definitely endearing, we wondered what it said about kindness. Is it just cute children, kittens, and puppies? Or something more? Why is it that when we hear a story about someone being kind, we are so amazed? Pleased, but amazed.

Kindness is not always easy to find in today's world. Although we are more connected than ever technologically, it feels sometimes like we are more distant than ever from the human side. We live in a fast lane typified by a hyperactive environment with a twenty-four-hour news cycle that we can't escape, divisive discourse across our nation, and precious little time for reflection. It's no wonder that we see less and less kindness abound. Life is hard, and it got tougher after the arrival of the pandemic.

The truth is that the people we care about—our families, our friends, and those we work with—are more stressed, lonely, and afraid than ever. Life has changed significantly, and if ever there was a time for kindness, it is now. As human beings, we may be hardwired for survival, but we're also hardwired for belonging. Our longing for kindness is real. We know it when we see it, and we know it when we don't. And both impact us in important ways.

The types of unkind acts we witness on a daily basis are far too numerous to list here. They may involve macroaggressions, verbal or nonverbal behaviors intended to demean or disgrace someone. They may be the more covert microaggressions, which come in the form of smears, insults, or derogatory analogies. Making assumptions based on gender and sexist humor are unkind; so is poor listening. And sometimes unkindness is simply not noticing, being insensitive to the needs of others, or not saying thank you.

Researchers know that when we are a victim of unkind acts, we enter neural shutdown. We become more defensive and less open. As a simple example, if you're in a meeting where the boss cuts you off in the middle of an explanation and derisively rolls her eyes about the data that you just presented, you're embarrassed. You've been openly demeaned, and it's even worse if others are present. Welcome to the neural shutdown phase. Couple this with a possible microaggression based on gender ("Men never understand feelings. Women aren't fit for that type of work"), and the situation worsens.

We instantly become less creative, less innovative, and less likely to contribute. In short, we go into protective mode.

Absence of kindness impacts in other ways as well. In a number of studies over the years, scientists have shown that when we witness unkind acts, we enter the same neural shutdown phase as if we were the victims. Further, the impact can stay with us for days afterward, reducing our ability to think clearly, problem-solve, and be creative. Studies of individuals witnessing unkindness paint a picture of psychologically traumatized minds that take time to recover. This means that the boss who just yelled at you in the meeting impacted not only you but everyone else as well.

Kindness looks like, well, kindness. The Dalai Lama once said to be kind whenever possible. He further stated, "It is always possible." Those in leadership roles are morally obligated to nurture cultures of kindness in the workplace. It can be as simple as a knowing glance to someone who needs to be acknowledged. It can be a smile or touch of a hand, or really listening. Sometimes it's about tone of voice, or eye contact, or a simple nonverbal nod to another. Kind acts are unlimited in their variety and immeasurable in their impact on others.

When we're kind to one another, the impact is truly at the cellular level—not the phone, the body. Think biology. Studies show that kindness has the ability to improve both our physiological and our psychological well-being. Immune systems are strengthened, and stress levels are lowered through acts of kindness. We feel better and are healthier. We think more clearly. We're happier. And according to a study in the journal *Emotion*, people who were treated with kindness at work were 287 percent more generous (Chancellor et al. 2018). Kindness breeds more kindness.

Organizationally, the effects of kindness multiply exponentially. Kind acts generate a positive organizational vibe that improves job satisfaction, increases productivity, and reduces turnover. The workplace becomes more sensitive, accepting, and engaged. People are perceived as more civil, more competent, and warmer. Meetings become more vibrant as people feel free to share their ideas. Our most valuable assets, people, feel safe from ridicule or targeting.

For leaders, it's not that difficult to be kind, and humility is a good place to start. Jim Collins's groundbreaking book *Good to Great: Why Some Companies Make the Leap . . . and Others Don't* found that one of the two most consistent traits among leaders who took companies from good to great was humility (Collins 2001). Humility bridges the gap between senior and junior folks in an organization. As such, it's the perfect entrée into love. Being sensitive to tone of voice and personal space matters as well. Both can send strong messages of encouragement and support. Finally, embracing noble intent matters. When we assume that people are coming from a place of goodness, we set the stage for kindness to abound.

Time for another seemingly stray comment that actually applies to the book. One of the authors drives a Jeep, and he's nuts about it—oops, we gave away which one. Anyway, it's an old candy-apple-red Jeep with no air-conditioning. One of the best things about this vehicle is not the open-air feel, or the big tires, or the peace-sign bumper sticker, it's the Jeep Wave—a time-honored practice for Jeep drivers across the country. Urban Dictionary defines this tradition as follows:

> An honor bestowed upon those drivers with the superior intelligence, taste, class, and discomfort tolerance (exception to 97 and newer Jeep owners) to own the ultimate vehicle—the Jeep. Generally consists of either a raised hand waving or 4 fingers extended upward from the steering wheel, but may be modified to suit circumstances and locally accepted etiquette (Urban Dictionary 2008).

What we like most about the Jeep Wave is that no matter what's happening in life, one can always count on a friendly wave from a stranger, or more than one if your commute is a bear. A friendly gesture that can make a bad day not so bad. It's a genuine act of kindness, beautiful in its simplicity and powerful in its effect. This is the hallmark of what kindness is. Simple, impactful. Leaders don't underestimate the power of kindness. It's unpretentious, it's unassuming, and it's a strong foundation for love.

Organizational Impact of Love

With all the focus in recent years on metrics, productivity tools, and technology, it might come as a surprise that the evidence of the impact of love in the workplace is astonishing. But not to us! Organizations are transformed when they are led by people who put love out there as their primary focus. Just look at Dawn's and Arthur's successes.

Research undeniably supports the impact of love in the workplace. In a landmark study, "What's Love Got to Do with It? A Longitudinal Study of the Culture of Companionate Love and Employee and Client Outcomes in a Long-Term Care Setting," Wharton professors Sigal Barsade and Olivia A. O'Neill found that staff who considered their organizational culture to be one of care and love were more satisfied in their jobs. They also reported higher levels of teamwork and took fewer days off. And get this, the findings were the same regardless of industry (Barsade and O'Neill 2014a). People want to love and be loved. Barsade and O'Neill's results are typical of what the vast majority of research has uncovered about the presence of love in leadership. Stronger cultures, more engagement, greater productivity—you get the idea. And there's more:

- **People who work in places of love may live longer.** One twenty-year study, controlling for behaviors that may serve to shorten the average life span, found that those with strong peer social support (aka love) lived longer (Shirom et al. 2011). C'mon, man, this is what we're about as human beings: love, support, compassion.
- **Teams are tighter.** Not just teams, people. When people in the workplace are bonded by love, they forge solid bonds with one another that keep them together. This is especially advan-

tageous during the stressful times of organizational change or adversity. People feel they can lean on and turn to each other in difficult times.

- **The culture is more forgiving.** Don't get us started on this. By and large, our work environments are not accepting of mistakes, or even exploratory inquiry. The presence of love helps foster an environment where forgiveness and assumption of noble intent is the norm, not the exception. Casual slights are easily overlooked. Personal sensitivity is not at an all-time high. And this has the ability to lead to . . .

- **Organizations that are more human.** Organizations are not charts—they are people. Sadly, we don't always view them that way. By their very nature, they run the risk of becoming impersonal entities with no soul. When love is present, when care for one another rules, and when there's an abundance of empathy, organizations take on the very human qualities toward which we should all strive. And don't think for a minute that the bottom line isn't impacted in a positive way. Why? See the next bullet!

- **People perform better.** Now we're talkin'. There's an old saying that when you love your job, you'll never work a day in your life. It's true. And the same is true with leaders who love, leaders who inspire. They create environments of commitment and caring that allow productivity to flourish. One study found that those working in an environment of affection, tenderness, caring, and compassion for one another held themselves more accountable for their own performance (Barsade and O'Neill 2014b).

- **There's more "we" than "me."** Love enhances the feeling of "us" along with a sense of purpose. People bound together in a common pursuit of organizational values and goals come together in a unique way. They have a magical sense of purpose that transcends personal gain.

- **People trust one another.** An environment of love increases the atmosphere of trust. Paul J. Zak, director of the Center for Neuroeconomics Studies at Claremont Graduate University, has done significant research in the area of workplace trust, and his findings suggest that organizations where trust prevails have more energy, engagement, and productivity. In fact, his work shows that if an organization improves trust by as little as one quartile, it results in an average of $10,185 in additional annual revenue (Zak 2017).
- **A positive emotional culture emerges.** Emotional capital is crucial for relationships. One study over eighteen industries showed that cultures of love and joy had a positive impact on employee-organization relationships (Men 2017). When joy, happiness, excitement, compassion, affection, love, and warmth were present, and driven by leadership, it allowed for compassion, forgiveness, joy, and nonjudgmental communication. Sounds like a good place to work to us!

OK, now that we've hooked you on this idea of love, we must confess that there are always barriers within organizations that do not allow for the free flow of love that we espouse. Organizational culture, past practices, groupthink, toxicity, fear, and lack of trust are among the more common. But personal barriers are present as well. They're significant, and they deserve attention.

Parker Palmer refers to the masks we wear, and it's so true. We all wear them sometimes. It may be the mask of the supervisor, the boss, the scientist, the technician. We may wear the mask of the patient boss when we're not; the good listener when we're not; or the know-it-all, which we never are. We wear the mask we want others to see. There is no breaking through these masks. They hide us from others and hide us from who we are. When we wear them in the workplace, we are not being authentic, and we shield ourselves from true connections with those with whom we work.

Sometimes the masks we wear originate from personal experiences that have hampered our ability to be intimate with one another. A history of lies or abuse, personally or professionally, can leave lasting scars on the human soul and make us reticent to offer or receive love. Orphanages are often notorious for deaths not related to starvation or disease, but to the emotional and sensory deprivation that is spawned from a lack of love (Varela-Silva 2016). Our response to such trauma as adults is often unconscious, and it takes tremendous self-awareness work to heal these wounds. In the meantime, we push love away. M. Scott Peck asserted that the question of love was the foundation of all the challenges his patients faced. His perspective was that the key ingredient of meaningful psychotherapy was love (Peck 1978).

When these struggles manifest themselves in the workplace, they can take the form of nonproductive behavior at best and toxic behavior at worst. Leaders unable to shed their masks become barriers to inclusion and progressive decision-making. They consciously or unconsciously block progress so as to maintain their sense of self-value. In extreme cases, and all too commonly, toxic behavior may emerge, creating an environment of workplace incivility and leaving little room for love.

So, Try This

- Think about the work-related documents that tell others what your organization is about. Do they explicitly mention love?
- Listen closely to the conversations you witness in the workplace. Think about how many of them you would characterize as exchange-based versus human-based.
- When was the last time you exhibited empathy to someone who worked for you? Was it in person? Emails don't count! Did you feel a genuine love for that person, or was this a professional encounter? Were you checking a box, or was it real?

And Finally

We would be remiss if we didn't close this chapter by making the point that love begins with self. We have to be able to look in the mirror in the morning and like what we see. Actually, love what we see, with all of our faults, imperfections, and scars. Leaders who are comfortable with self have the strongest foundation for leadership possible. This is why it is not possible to certify one's self into leadership. All of the great programs in the world, degrees, certifications, licensures, cannot fix a broken self, a self with no love.

When leaders begin with a foundation of authentic love for self, it is much easier to share love with others. Leaders like this are the real deal. Think about Dawn and Arthur. Because they were their true selves, they were able to impact those they led and all of those around them. They led with love. You could too.

PART II

LAUGHTER

CHAPTER 4

WHY LAUGH?

We don't trust stairs.
They're always up to something!

And that's just how bad this chapter is likely to be, but don't blame us. You purchased the book. And now you get exposure to jokes like you've never seen. OMG—this just might be our favorite chapter! Let's get started already!

We see you smiling.

We laugh at many things. Not enough, but many. Stand-up comedians can have us laughing so hard we hurt. Our friends can't wait to tell us a joke they heard. We giggle at the cute comments that children utter. All can evoke a chuckle. Twitter feeds are pretty entertaining too. There seems to be no end to the amusing intellect of many in our communities. We even laugh when we're nervous. Most of us know that one coworker or friend who seems to laugh as part of his speaking voice when under pressure or uses nervous laughter as a coping mechanism.

If by this point you've decided to express more love in your leadership, that's terrific. Love is universally accepted as a good thing, and crossing the line where love is concerned is a lot clearer for most. Love cannot truly be viewed as hostile, antagonistic, or degrading, but laughter can. Those who laugh too much may be seen as insensitive or as the office clowns who take nothing seriously, or who turn things around and claim it was only a joke. Humor can offend and can turn sour very quickly.

The contrast between laughter and love is truly striking, which is what makes them such a great combination for leaders to wield. Unlike love, which has largely been ignored or minimized in leadership because it doesn't fit into the latest modern-day leadership frameworks, laughter has been flat-out eschewed. Laughter carries risks. It can be a great icebreaker, or it can offend. Laughter can bring a room together or divide it down the middle.

Jokes and one-liners in the workplace also carry a few other burdens that love does not. Humor can be seen as witty, or it can be seen as juvenile and childish. And those who deliver the punchline or toss in a comical verbal remark may be appreciated as clever team members or pegged as unprofessional jokesters. After all, how can you be having fun and actually working hard?

Are you ready? Here comes the case for laughter—the history, the science, the risks, the benefits, and why it matters for leadership. And for the record, laughter and humor are different things. Laughter is a response to humor. Humor makes us laugh if it's funny. For the purposes of our exploration, we want to keep it simple, so we'll talk about both without getting into intellectual debates about how one works with the other. One prominent scholar, John Morreall, proposed that laughter is the consequence of a psychological change, but humor is the result of a cognitive adjustment (Morreall 1987). OK, cool. We agree, John, but let's not get too crazy. We need them both for leadership, period.

In order to lead with laughter and have a sense of humor, we need to understand it better. This is especially true when we want to be ourselves and just let go. We want to frame our passion for humor and how it makes us better as leaders, more relatable, and more effective. Laughing makes us feel good. And no fair jumping from joke to joke. Thou must readeth the text in-betweeneth—so say the authors.

A pair of jumper cables walk into a bar. The bartender says, "OK, I'll serve you, but don't start anything!"

The Concept of Laughter

Theorists, philosophers, and researchers have studied laughter throughout the centuries. There's no doubt that inquiry into the mystery of laughter has been reflected in the best efforts of sociologists, biologists, psychologists, anthropologists, historians, and stand-up comedians. Did cavepeople tell jokes to ease the day-to-day stress of, well, being a caveperson? Did they study history? Get it? History? Did cavepeople study history? C'mon, that was hilarious.

Not much is known about laughter and our earliest ancestors, but theories abound, from prehistoric guttural chuckles to our ancestors sharing stories by firelight to more substantive social connections. Scientists have suggested ape play as the evolutionary foundation of laughter. No, not your children tearing up the basement. The fact is, in those rare moments when apes felt safe, they bantered about in a manner that gave rise to modern laughter among humans. This "non-serious social incongruity," as it is called, became our contemporary playfulness. And once humans gained control over their facial motor systems, two million years ago, laughter was here to stay (Gervais and Wilson 2005).

As societies grew and communities became more complex, laughter and humor continued to permeate civilization. A 2008 study by the University of Wolverhampton even uncovered the world's oldest joke (McDonald 2013). It appears in Sumerian tablets from the Old Babylonian period and dates back to between 1900 and 2300 BC. And yes, it's potty humor. It's about flatulence, to be precise. It reads: "Something which has never occurred since time immemorial; a young woman did not fart in her husband's lap." We shall take a step away from recommending toilet humor for leaders. Even though *Potty Humor for Leaders* does seem like a pretty funny title for our next book. Don't worry—we won't. Well, one of us wants to, but, well. You get it.

The Egyptians are due a lot of credit for their love of humor and laughter. Archaeologists have uncovered hieroglyphic depictions of animals doing human things like driving chariots or playing board games, sort of a modern-day version of the Cassius Marcellus Coolidge painting of dogs playing poker. The Egyptians were also fans of satire, with artists of the time utilizing witty caricatures of queens and common folks alike.

The Greeks were pretty negative about laughter, maybe because they conquered Egypt in 332 BC and were a little jealous of the Egyptians' celebrated sense of humor. Of all of the grumpy Greeks, Plato was a real bummer. The dude loved love, but laughter, not so much. If you were the Greek equivalent of a worker at a Department of Motor Vehicles, aka a government employee, Plato considered laughter to be a huge no-no. He viewed laughter as cruel and irrational and not cool for public servants. And if you were a comedy writer, you were out of luck. In the words of Plato, "No composer of comedy, iambic or lyric verse shall be permitted to hold any citizen up to laughter, by word or gesture, with passion or otherwise" (Plato 1926). Ouch! Aristotle agreed. He wrote that wit was nothing more than educated insolence (Aristotle and Roberts 2004). Double ouch!

As far as the Romans? Now we're talking. Our toga-laden citizen friends lay claim to what many consider the oldest surviving joke book. Philogelos, loosely translated as "The One Who Loves Laughter" or "The Joker," was written in the fourth or fifth century BC, and it was no small endeavor. This book contained approximately 265 jokes. A prime example?

An idiot bumps into a friend and says, "I heard you had died!"
"Well, as you can see," replies the friend, "I am quite alive."
"But the guy who told me is so much more trustworthy than you!"—Crompton 2010

That's funny.

Even the political leaders of the time got in on the act, albeit with some reservations. Remember we're talking about ancient Rome, and there could be a heavy price to pay for angering the wrong pre-

Did you know that parrots are laughing at us and other pets in the home? In forums for parrot owners, it was recalled that Mariam Rothschild's parrot would whistle and call, by name, her dog into the room, and when the dog came into the room, it would laugh out loud. Seriously, laugh! A pet store employee also claimed that as she swept up around the parrot cages at the end of the day, one of the parrots in the store would wait until she was finished and then go over to the food dish and, using its beak, push and throw the food seeds on the floor, and—you guessed it—laugh! It's the same type of humor as when a friend comes to pick you up and, just as you are about to grab the car door to open it, drives forward—just a little—so that you have to take another step . . . and yes, repeats the same "game." Not recommended for the office.

fect. According to Mary Beard's book *Laughter in Ancient Rome: On Joking, Tickling, and Cracking Up*, Julius Caesar took a comedic beating from his colleagues for his comb-over. Turns out making fun of baldness was in the "OK" category for Romans (Beard 2014). Accepting a joke with humor and grace was a necessity, but it also had a more treacherous side, as did so many things in ancient Rome.

Beyond the Romans, laughter took various twists and turns on the way to modern times. In the twelfth century and into the Middle Ages, laughter became a powerful force and many times came at the expense of others. It was used politically as a divisive tool and to belittle groups. It's described both as wholesome and as damning. But it was also prevalent in happier moments, as a way to ease stress, as a coping mechanism, and as a way to build camaraderie. In the United States, laughing was viewed in our earliest history in much the same vein as by Aristotle—imprudent and a sign of low intelligence.

Fast-forward to 1871, and things started to look up. *Puck*—the magazine, not the chef (love his pizza)—appeared seemingly from out of nowhere, bringing a welcome respite to days plagued by drab clothing and endless work. From 1871 to 1918, this German-language humor magazine, founded by Joseph Keppler, offered Americans a dose of political satire, anecdotes, and colorful, detailed cartoons confronting the issues of the times. Nothing was off-limits, and the graphic humor depicted in the magazine included social movements, religion, politicians, and more. Other publications quickly followed, including *Vanity Fair*, *Life*, *Judge*, and *The California Pelican*. And what about those college campuses? They were poking fun as early as 1872 on the campus of Yale, and many are still in print, including *The Harvard Lampoon*, *The Stanford Chaparral*, *The Yale Record*, *The Pennsylvania Punch Bowl*, and *The Princeton Tiger*.

Two muffins are sitting in an oven. One muffin looks at the other and says, "Hey, man, sure is hot in here." The second muffin looks over and exclaims, "Oh my gosh, it's a talking muffin!"

What Happens When We Laugh and When We Don't

There is no shortage of opinions about why we human beings laugh. When we look at laughter over the years, it is most commonly thought to come out of *superiority*, *relief*, and *incongruity*. Sounds boring right? But actually it makes sense, and when viewed through the leadership lens, it makes a lot of sense!

Superiority

So, you're in a meeting with your colleagues, and the boss, Iris, steps in to join the discussion. Up until that moment, the communication back and forth in the meeting had been both constructive and productive. Her arrival is met with a collective suck of the oxygen out of the room. Sure enough, within minutes, she says something like "I'm sure glad you all are having fun—wish I had time for jokes!"

followed by a demeaning chortle. And worse? She picks on those she knows won't fight back.

Iris's actions reflect the superiority theory of laughter and mirror the ancient Greeks' perspective on humor. She brings with her a dark cloud of doubt that covers the room and all within. People in the meeting expect this and they shut down, wondering if they will be the next victim of her cynical barbs. What she does, and what so many poor leaders do, is accommodate their own inadequacies by making snide comments or using lingo only they understand. This is dominance pure and simple—the opposite of what we are talking about in this book.

Both Plato and Aristotle depict perspectives of supremacy and authority in the use of humor. English philosopher Thomas Hobbes described superiority well by equating such laughter with the elevated feeling of self we experience "by comparison with the infirmity of others, or with our own formerly" (Hobbes 1840). What the heck is he saying? He's saying that Iris is choosing, deliberately, to put down people in the room to raise her status or compensate for her own lack of self-esteem. She's seeking what Hobbes calls "glory" in her aggressive action. She places herself above others. She dominates. Welcome to the dark side of laughter. Something to think about the next time you experience this.

Relief

You're in another meeting at work. The team has been toiling away on Project X for months now. Overtime has been the norm, but you can see the finish line ahead. You're probably no more than three days away from completion and some well-earned time off. Michael, one of the project leads, returns from a meeting with the director. As he walks in the room, he appears glum. "They've changed everything! They want us to start from scratch with new parameters! We have to start all over!" The room goes silent as everyone tries to digest the terrible news. "I'm just kidding!" Michael says. Everyone cracks up as they realize he was joking.

What happened above was laughter that arose from relief. The team did not laugh at something that was actually humorous, as in the muffin joke above. They laughed out of a release of suppressed energy, the energy of disbelief that things had changed so dramatically. The room must have been in a state of focus, given the task at hand, as often happens in the workplace. When Michael made his announcement, the team was flabbergasted that something so dramatic could have happened. Minds begin to race. "What's going on?" "Where did this come from?" "How could they do this to us?" Once Michael came clean, people were relieved!

Relief theory stems from our early assessments of the physiological expression of laughter—the expelled breath, our body bouncing, our eyes watering, the guttural sounds emerging—and was influenced by our early perceptions of the nervous system. As such, the concept of relief suggests that laughter may be a sort of release valve for pent-up emotions in humans. So, funny has nothing to do with it.

Relief theory has been a controversial topic among researchers in their attempt to explain the puzzle of laughter. Still, many philosophers and scientists over the years found credibility in the approach. Sigmund Freud supported relief theory and tied it to all sorts of psychological complexities, including release of psychic energy, hostility, repression, and sexual feelings (no shock there—it's Freud, after all!).

Incongruity

You're in a meeting at work (wow, you attend a lot of meetings), but this is a big meeting. The head of the company, Jordan, is going to address the group to talk about the future direction of the organization. Everyone is curious how this will go. Most don't know Jordan, but she comes off as quite formal and all business. She's not a handshake-and-smile kind of person, but she is honest and direct. As her assistant introduces her, she walks into the room wearing Groucho Marx glasses, complete with the mustache. Everyone busts out in giggles.

Jordan nailed this one. Good for her! And many kudos for being self-aware enough to know that her little prank would be so impactful, given her normal demeanor. Jordan knew she needed to garner some positive attention and create a relaxed atmosphere, and she did so with style and an understated manner. No need to tell a joke, even though that may have worked as well. Nope. She knew that something as outrageous as Groucho Marx glasses would do the trick. No words needed. Just arrival in the room. Brilliant.

Incongruity theory is a comedian's best friend. When Amy Schumer nails the punchline on a joke, it catches the audience off guard. What seemed to make sense no longer applies. Our expectations are thwarted, and we are introduced to an unexpected outcome. Our brains go in overdrive trying to refocus on where we thought things were going and how we ended up where we did. Voilà, a joke is born! Even though this theory was introduced in the late nineteenth century, there is evidence of this idea much earlier. Aristotle writes of generating an expectation with an audience and then altering course in order to evoke laughter. Kant also makes reference to the basis of incongruity theory by suggesting that laughter arises with the expectation that is transformed into nothing (Kant 1951).

Superiority, relief, and incongruity theories aside, laughter brings us together. This is one of the most agreed-upon tenets of laughter: it builds social connections. As life became more complex and as civilizations grew, laughter was one of the great bonds. It allowed for socialization and play, even in the darkest of times. So, sometimes laughter is about humor, and sometimes it helps us build our social networks. One thing everyone agrees on is that laughter is everywhere, in all societies, across species, in every culture. It may look and sound different, and certainly what we find funny differs, but it's there. Why not in leadership?

Laughter lets me relax. It's the equivalent of
taking a deep breath, letting it out, and saying,
"This, too, will pass." —Odette Pollar

The Physiology of Laughter

The funniness landscape is a bleak one, especially if we compare daily laughter between an adult and a child. Scientists observe that an average four-year-old laughs as many as three hundred times per day, at everything from sights to sounds. Adults laugh far less, with some estimates at up to fifteen times per day. And no, "LOL" in your text messaging doesn't count. Sadly, it is a fact that we laugh less as we age, and less during the weekdays.

It helps that we enjoy laughing, even if we don't do it enough. We laugh differently, at different things, at different ages. We laugh one way if we're being tickled and another if we're doing the tickling. *(Authors' really important note: Tickling is not recommended as a leadership practice. And as important as we think laughter is, we do not advocate physical tickling in the workplace! BUT . . . since we brought it up anyway, it's worth a mention because no one understands why we laugh when we're tickled.)* The opus of our respiratory muscles, voice, larynx, and nasal passages creates a laughing sound as unique as our fingerprint. It may be a chortle, a guffaw, or a snort, but they're all funny, especially the snort.

Our outward physical reaction to humor is funny in and of itself, but the complex neurodynamics tied to laughter are even more fascinating. We can think of the brain's task in laughter as containing three crucial pieces: recognizing and understanding the emotions related to humor, the cognitive aspect of "getting" the joke, and the motor component that fuels our physical reaction. All three of these are required in order for us to physically laugh.

In groundbreaking research, Peter Derks and a team of scientists at William and Mary College were able to track the electrical circuitry of the brain as individuals laughed. They observed that several parts of the brain are responsible for the ability to produce laughter. The cortex plays a role in dissecting the organization of the joke itself, including the word selection. It also performs the computation necessary to recognize the humor in the joke. The frontal and occipital lobes get into the act by weighing social and emotional factors and processing visual signals. This neural activity, combined with the limbic system, helps us recognize and control our behaviors and expression of mood (Derks et al. 1997).

As the primary motor cortex generates the nerve impulses that cause our movement, our respiratory system begins to engage. Fifteen different facial muscles, including the zygomaticus major muscle, allow a visible smile to begin forming. Airflow to the larynx is interrupted due to movement of the epiglottis, and before you know it, that small giggle has become an outright howl. Ultimately, the hypothalamus helps generate our ability for irrepressible laughter. Our face or neck turns red, and tears may even start to flow. We are in full laughter mode!

The outward physical appearance of laughter is a mosaic unto itself. We've all witnessed different types of laughter, ranging from quiet to loud, still to demonstrative, and authentic to cynical. Sometimes we even laugh at people who are laughing. Scientists have found that we laugh differently depending on the circumstances. When watching a funny movie alone, we may laugh, but not crazy out loud. But toss in a few friends watching the same flick, and the volume and intensity of the laugher increase. According to research by Robert Provine, we are 30 percent more likely to laugh in a social setting than when alone (Provine 2000). Hence the social-connectedness value of laughter!

I have always felt that laughter in the face of reality is probably the finest sound there is and will last until the day when the game is called on account of darkness. In this world, a good time to laugh is any time you can. —Linda Ellerbee

When we do get to the point of outward laughter, the variety is astounding. Scientists have found that there may be as many as fifteen distinct types of such laughter: smirk, smile, grin, snicker, giggle, chuckle, chortle, laugh, cackle, guffaw, howl, shriek, roar, convulse, and die laughing—seriously, yes, the last one is die laughing (Kuhn 1994, as adapted by Berk 2001). Each of these grows exponentially, from an oh-so-slightly imperceptible lift of the corners of the mouth to an experience of breathlessness and exhaustion. Some kinds of laughter can be used for more nefarious reasons, such as smirking or snickering. Smirking, snickering, and smiling are more controllable than the others, but giggling becomes the gateway to big laughs because there's a 50 percent chance that it will evolve into full-fledged laughter.

A man with a carrot stuck in his ear and a piece of celery in his nose walks into a doctor's office. He says, "Doctor, doctor, I'm not feeling well." The doctor says, "I know what the problem is: you're not eating right."

When we laugh, we're happier. When we're happier, we laugh more, and our laughter spawns laughter in those around us. So, lots of good things happen when we laugh. But laughter is connected to far more than just happiness or creating laughter with others. It has significant benefits to the mind and body.

One of the more notable stories that show the impact of laughter on the human body and soul is that of author and professor Norman Cousins. As a researcher, Cousins had long advocated the importance of human emotion in combating illness and often argued that negative emotions would lead to bad physiological outcomes. Conversely, maintaining a positive mindset presented a better chance to lead to a positive result. In 1964, when he was diagnosed with ankylosing spondylitis, a painful and debilitating disease that can cause small bones in the spine to fuse together, he was able to put his theories to work.

As part of his self-prescribed treatment, Cousins began by persuading his physicians to prescribe high doses of intravenous vitamin C. Then he started watching funny television shows and movies. The laughter worked. Cousins subsequently described in detail how ten minutes of laughter allowed him to sleep pain free for two hours. He went on to live for twenty-six years after doctors had diagnosed his illness, and he successfully utilized laughter therapy later in life as he battled heart disease (Cousins 1979).

Cousins's story is an important one, because it demonstrates the potential for laughter and its impact on our lives. Not only did laughter provide Cousins with physical comfort, but also it fed his positive mental attitude, which propelled him through the rest of his life. It provided him with comfort in the face of a debilitating and painful disease, and the benefits of laughter on a personal level are indeed remarkable. The following are some examples.

Laughter Is a Workout

Not so fast! We can hear you canceling your gym memberships all over the country. But yes, it is. Recall that laughter is a full-body action. When we cut loose at the level of uncontrolled laughter, we're not only calling on muscles from the face, abdomen, legs, and back but also revving up our respiratory system and diaphragm. We won't go as far as to suggest that giggling can replace time on the elliptical, but laughter has been linked to benefits similar to those gained through exercise. In research at Vanderbilt University, Maciej Buchowski found that ten to fifteen minutes of hearty laughter expended as many as fifty calories (Buchowski et al. 2007). Let's put

Did you know that in studies in the animal kingdom, panting sounds that are made by chimps, bonobos, gorillas, and orangutans sound a lot like human laughter, and the likeness is determined by how closely related the primates are to humans? Panting by chimpanzees and bonobos sounds most like human laughter. A gorilla named Koko was famous for displaying some ability to joke around. Koko, who knew more than two thousand words and one thousand sign language signs, responded to the question "What can you think of that's hard?" by signing "rock" and "work." She also once was documented as playing with her trainer, tying her shoelaces together and signing the word "chase." Then she made laughing noises as her trainer tried walking around with the laces tied. LOL.

it into perspective: that's about the number of calories in a piece of chocolate. And now you know the secret to life: eat a piece of chocolate, laugh for fifteen minutes, eat another piece of chocolate, laugh for fifteen minutes, rinse and repeat. You're welcome.

Laughter Keeps You from Getting Sick

Laughter has been linked to improvements in our immune function. Scientists in the field of psychoneuroimmunology, which for the record is the longest word you'll see in this book and worth a gazillion points in Scrabble, have found significant connections between human emotions and their impact on our immune system. In one study published in the *American Journal of the Medical Sciences*, Lee Berk of Loma Linda University and William Fry of Stanford University performed a meta-analysis to determine whether laughter impacted the body's immune function. Fry got the tough part of the experiment: he was assigned the job of watching episodes of Laurel & Hardy and Abbott & Costello. Meanwhile, Berk ran samples on Fry's cortisol levels. They determined that laughter increased the production of cells that help the body fight infection (Berk et al. 1989).

Laughter Reduces Stress and Improves Vascular Health

And who doesn't need this? The majority of Americans consistently report being stressed, especially at work. Laughter has the potential to reduce those killer stress hormones, like cortisol, epinephrine, and DOPAC. In fact, the body does us a favor by dropping the levels of these hormones merely by anticipating laughter. One study showed that laughter can also improve the elasticity and function of blood vessels, protecting against cardiovascular disease. This happens because laughter causes the endothelium, the tissue that makes up the inner lining of blood vessels, to dilate and expand. This improves blood flow to the heart, lungs, and brain for as much as twenty-four hours after the laughter concludes.

Laughter Can Help Relieve Pain

Just ask Norman Cousins. Since his groundbreaking experience, more and more data have piled up suggesting that laughter allows our body to produce natural painkillers. Patients who watch funny videos are less likely to experience intense pain and less likely to need medication. Scientists posit that this is related to the release of endorphins. In one study, test participants viewed fifteen minutes of comedy and then were exposed to having their arm wrapped in a frozen wine-cooling sleeve or instructed to squat against a wall as long as they could. Their pain threshold was increased by 10 percent.

Laughter Improves Your Mental Health

So much. Everything from improving mood to clearing the mind to bonding with strangers. Laughter does it all. It can help us relax and sleep better, and even boost our memory. Cognitive neuroscientists say that laughing engages both sides of the brain, improving our ability to learn and our cognitive ability. When we make sophisticated connections necessary to understand a joke, we exercise our brain. We also become more creative in our thought patterns.

So here we are, making the same argument we made in your highlighted and marked-up version of chapter 1. Yes, we're hoping you're doing that—it means you like the book! Just as with love, what's not to like about laughter? It drives social bonding and has done so since our species appeared on the planet five to seven million years ago. It lightens difficult situations. And thanks to the amazing physiological miracle that is the human body, giggling at a one-liner makes us physically and mentally healthier. We need to laugh, and it's a good thing that we do. And since we do, why wouldn't it be a part of our leadership as well?

> *A leader walks into an empty bar. She has just completed a difficult day of meetings and is happy to have a little alone time. As she enjoys her beer, she hears a voice from out of*

nowhere say, "Nice jacket!" She looks around and sees no one. "Nice Louboutins too!" the voice says. She calls the bartender over and asks where the voice is coming from. "It's the peanuts," he says. "They're complimentary!"

When Laughter Is Missing in Leadership

The roar of the laughter out there is killing us, but we must press on. Still more of the book to go! And how ironic that many are still making the same arguments against laughter that were made against love, as recounted in the first chapter.

Zina and Patrick, it's not professional.

Zina and Patrick, we have to have boundaries in the workplace.

Zina and Patrick, I run a tight ship.

Yeah, we heard these somewhere before. Recall those thinking patterns that keep us on the straight and narrow? And those pesky but attractive graphics and terms that continue to make the case for serious words like *courage* and *resilience* in leadership? Yes—they help, and they're good. But they envelop us in artificial constructs that cloud our ability to see laughter and love for what they are: foundational. Truly foundational. This is where we begin. Everything grows from there.

Laughter allows for a relaxed and creative workplace. We'll get into more details on this later, but for now let's focus on what leadership is like when humor is not present. Bottom line? It's ugly, and it can get uglier fast. And let's be honest, in today's work environments, the wicked mixture of internally imposed deadlines, resource shortages, external pressures, and personality conflicts makes for a less-than-perfect environment for comedic fun. Fair enough. But when humor is missing, so are some of the most important talents needed to compete in a hyper-competitive environment.

First and foremost, leaders with no sense of humor struggle to engage with their workforce. Engagement has been pretty much at the top of the "what leaders fail to do" list for the last several years. The "just get your job done" approach may work temporarily, but it won't last, and it's not leadership. It's coercion. One of the most impactful steps a leader can take is a simple foray into relaxing, letting go, and innocent humor. A simple self-effacing comment can bring a leader immediately to the level of those she leads. The approachability factor skyrockets, and people are more easily able to feel at one with the leader. The resulting side effects of trust and connection are priceless.

Another consideration is the environment that may be present if humor is missing. It doesn't take long for a workplace to go from professional to toxic. Not that professional is bad in and of itself. We count on professionalism in our workplaces, to a point. It helps us with our processes, but its impact on relationships and culture is greatly overrated. It's important to note that we weren't born to be professional, we were born to love and laugh. And professional organizations so often miss the boat on real human relationships. So, if the organization has slipped from professional to toxic, buyer beware! Lack of accountability, divisiveness, and even lawsuits are sure to follow. Trust, the lubrication of all organizations, will be nonexistent. There may be no coming back from that.

Against the assault of laughter, nothing can stand. —Mark Twain

Team building? Fuggedaboutit! It's far harder to build effective teams in businesses that aren't fun to work in. Hear this: the organization of today doesn't need heroes! It requires mission-focused teams marked by passion, engagement, energy, and talent. Let's face it, leading the development of these teams is one of the most important skills a leader can have, but it doesn't happen easily. Each team member brings his or her own ego, talents, fears, and eccentricities. But the ability to bring team members together is greatly aided in an environment marked by laughter. People feel more comfortable with one another. Humor is the connective tissue for these groups, allowing familiarity, cohesion, and comfort. And guess what? When conflict occurs, it's far easier to address.

Did you know that your dog may very likely have a sense of humor? A University of California, Davis, study took a look at different dog breeds and ranked them based on their playfulness, assuming that dogs who were eager to participate in activities were probably the ones exhibiting humor through play. Ever play tug of war with a dog and his toy? You let go; he holds on for a bit; and then, very slowly, he lets it go free while hovering over it just enough to give you the feeling that you can make a dash for it, while he almost joyfully and playfully waits for you to reach down and grab it again. And when you think you are going to make away with that toy, he grabs it once again, silently laughing at you like the 1960s cartoon character Muttley. Dog humor? Maybe! Some of the highest jovial scores were for Irish setters, springer spaniels, standard poodles, and cairn terriers.

Finally, environments unmarked by a little fun not only are less productive but also have poorer retention. No one likes working in a grumpy place. No one. When the work environment is complete with positive vibes, people feel good. About themselves. About the place where they work. About the work they do. When this happens, their passion is rekindled. Since humor leads to positive emotions, and positive emotions make individuals feel good, they naturally communicate better, become more committed team members, and work harder. This also improves retention, since happy, productive workers are less likely to leave their jobs.

So why wouldn't leaders embrace laughter? You'll recall that in chapter 1, we identified six types of leaders and the reasons for their aversion to love. Guess what? The same applies to humor. Let's take a quick peek and see what they look like through the lens of laughter:

The "I Got This" leader. Since this leader is so confident of her past experiences and knowledge base, don't expect much in the way of humor unless it's an old, forced joke. We'll see this leader again later!

The "Catchphrase" leader. Not going to happen. Leadership by acronym never includes humor.

The "Selfie" leader. Well, actually, yeah. Unfortunately, the comicality is likely to be designed to put someone in their place or embarrass them. Think smirk.

The "Call Me by My Title" leader. Nope. Too focused on status to ever let loose enough for jocularity.

The "Show Me the Metrics" leader. Only if they read this book. Can't deny the data!

The "I Don't Even Like Myself" leader. Still sad, and unfortunately this leader isn't comfortable enough with who they are to go out on the vulnerability limb, where comedy is concerned.

To be fair, humor can be tricky, so don't be too hard on the folks above. But the love of laughter is present from the earliest time of our lives, and with a little bit of sensitivity and care, laughter can become a powerful part of our leadership. It's part of being the real you, being human first.

So, Try This

- Keep a log of how often you laughed in a twenty-four-hour period. Distinguish between incongruity, relief, and superiority. How did you do it, and what do you think this tells you about yourself and your relationship with laughter?
- Take a look at work documents like mission statements, values, and team norms. Is the word *fun* anywhere? What about that leadership philosophy? See it there? Consider why not.
- In a moment of honest self-awareness, think about what you would use as self-deprecating humor. How vulnerable are you willing to be? Can you be humble? Try it sometime.

How You Know You Are Letting Go and Getting Real

- How are *you* feeling? Do the big issues and problems feel a bit less daunting and life-consuming? Are you able to recover from a let-down or failure a bit more quickly?
- How is your team interacting? When you walk by a team meeting or a few of your staff in the hall, or when people are waiting for everyone else to enter the videoconference call, are they sharing laughable moments that they have been experiencing either at home or with the work task? Are people laughing with each other? Countering one funny story with another?
- How is your team interacting with you? Are they coming to you with smiles on their faces and sharing close-call mishaps? Are you receiving way-off-the-wall and creative and sometimes quite funny solutions to problems? Are you coming up with the same?

And Finally

You probably didn't know that laughter had such a colorful history. Maybe the Egyptians foretold something we finally understand: laughter is a good thing. Like love, laughter is a crucial component for social connection. It brings together the most disparate of individuals, bonding us in a collective smile. If you think love is missing from the know-it-all theories of leadership, try doing a word search on the words *fun* or *joke* or *laugh*. Don't hold your breath.

When we laugh, we unleash physical, mental, and chemical reactions that help us cope with even the most difficult workplace. The result is clearer thinking, more innovation, and teams ready to tackle anything that comes their way. When it's fun, it's not work. And that's cool.

CHAPTER 5

LEADERS WHO MAKE US LAUGH

Whew, this will be a tough one. First of all, one of your authors can't stop laughing as she reads stories about funny leaders. One of the leaders she read about left a cute drawing on a sticky note to a subordinate that said: "Don't freak out. I believe in you. Somewhat." Another crazy character held an ugly-sweater contest but taped a mirror to the front of his sweater. Another put a potato filter on her virtual platform, which made her face look like a potato. The video went viral. You'll read more about her later. And the list goes on. We may never finish this chapter!

Laughter and humor, as we explored in the previous chapter, has a long and storied history, and their absence in the workplace makes for a pretty humdrum environment—boring, to say the least. We know that funny leaders exist out there. We know there are leaders out there who bring their whole selves to work, and that includes their humorous side. Sergey Brin, cofounder of Google, was apparently quite the card in a legitimate comedic fashion. Minnesota senator and Democratic presidential primary candidate Amy Klobuchar also shares a reputation for having precise comedic timing and self-deprecating humor. Likewise, Tony Hsieh, former CEO of Zappos, was known for his lighthearted approach to fun in the workplace.

One thing we know these individuals have in common is that they benefit their organizations by creating spaces that allow for the laughter, lightheartedness, and joy that people need in their lives. They allow for the whole person to be nurtured and cared for in the workplace. Because they meet these needs, and their own needs for laughter and joy, productivity, performance, and success increase, not just for the organization but for individuals as well. These leaders leave behind a legacy of accomplishments and goal attainment, and in some cases memories that are retained for a lifetime.

Leaders such as these, with a keen sense of humor, are accomplished, have high standards, hold employees accountable, coach, develop, and serve as role models. You too can be one of these leaders by embracing a little comedy, being courageous, being humble, being able to laugh at yourself with others, and having the social awareness to understand when and how to provide this safe space where the humor is appropriate and not offensive. It's about truly letting go of some of the uptightness with which we carry ourselves. When people can laugh together, a bond is created by that experience, a closeness, a trust. Laughter creates a communal space and a feeling of belonging. Employees and bosses become part of the same team.

As author and professor Don Zauderer once noted, one of the greatest accomplishments of an organization is to build a community where people feel included and welcomed (Zauderer 2002). When this occurs, people work together with mutual respect to enhance individual and organizational productivity. This is the kind of environment that builds a synergistic, collective vigor that attracts and retains quality talent. Humor does just that.

Let's take a look at a couple of leaders who are very successful, accomplished, and respected in their fields, and who will admit that they do bring their authentic selves to work, including their humorous side. They are able to laugh at themselves, with others, and can tap into the funny side of a situation. They are comfortable with the risks. They know this opens the door to bringing joy to others and giving them permission to not take themselves or work so seriously.

Our Laugh Heroes

Laugh Hero #1

Let's begin with what started one of us laughing so hard that we had to stop everything and share what we just saw, which interrupted the writing flow of the other, who almost missed an editorial deadline, but that's a different story! The potato boss. Yes, this is an actual thing. You can find it on the internet. Look up Lizet Ocampo.

Picture a high-level director holding Monday-morning meetings via video with her entire team. The staff are joining the online meeting, coffee in hand, ready to kick off another busy week. When they log in, and their director turns on her video, she has been transformed into a potato, planted in the dirt, with only her eyes and lips visible as the face of the potato. Think Mrs. Potato Head from back in the day! The director tries to remove the filter and has no luck. Potato eyes are darting across the screen as she desperately seeks the right key to remove this troublesome filter.

Everyone, including the director, cannot stop laughing at the image. As she speaks, her lips are moving and her eyes continue darting all over the screen, sometimes making the poor potato look sad as she struggles to clear the filter. She decides, in that moment, to simply continue the meeting . . . as a potato. This wasn't planned, and we don't know how many computers had to be replaced as her staff spewed coffee through their noses, but the director's reaction and resulting decision is the best part of this story.

The next day, a staff member posted a photo on Twitter with the caption "My boss accidentally turned herself into a potato and held the meeting anyway." The tweet went viral, with over forty-five million views and likes. And the director? She was cool with it. Now, for the record, we don't recommend that anyone take photos of private meetings and post anything without permission, but this accident brought out the best in the team. They saw their boss in a different light and realized that it was OK to laugh. The staff member was so glad her boss found it hilarious and noted how terrific it was being part of a team with such camaraderie, in spite of the pandemic.

Lizet Ocampo, the political director of People For the American Way, is a first-generation American whose parents immigrated to the United States from Mexico as farmworkers. They are very proud of their daughter! Interestingly, they were pleased not only because she graduated from Stanford University, worked on presidential campaigns, worked in Congress and the White House, and helped others to find and reach their dreams, but mostly because of what happened in her first job outside of college, at Google. What made her parents so proud was that while at Google, Lizet had access to free food. Food was not plentiful in the Campos household. Working at Google gave her parents a sense of comfort that Lizet would always be OK.

Early in her career, Lizet was fortunate to work for amazing leaders. She soaked in all that she saw, including how to hold people accountable, manage high expectations, and ensure mission accomplishment. She put in long hours, found time to volunteer, and learned early on that fun and passion for her cause were easily compatible. She was blessed with bosses who started their meetings with jokes, and to this day, she starts her Monday meetings by asking if anyone has a funny story or fun experience to share from the weekend.

Is she successful? Oh yeah. She graduated from Stanford; went to work at Google; worked in Washington, DC, for the U.S. Senate; ended up at the White House working for the Obama administration; and is now serving as the political director for People For the American Way. Her staff members describe her as not only fun and real, a person who recognizes and nurtures the whole person, but also someone who has high standards and expectations. Holding people accountable is still part of her persona. She knows this, but she also recognizes that others may be in situations that need her to coach, educate, and guide. She does this while allowing herself and her team to find joy in the workplace, and to laugh and own experiences that allow her to be human and accept the human in others. She learned part of that lesson from the Obamas.

Lizet recalls a time when she was working at the White House, sometimes spending twenty hours a day with her team, and she had an experience with the president and his family where she learned three valuable lessons: life is unpredictable, there is room for the whole person at work, and laughter comes with being real. Since she often traversed the path between the East and West Wings of the White House, it was not unusual for her to walk through the private residence on a daily basis. One day she did just that, at the exact time when the first family was meeting their new puppy Bo. Not knowing that this was happening and it was being photographed, she walked right in! Immediately, Bo ran over to her, sniffing, circling, and wagging his tail. Unsure of what to do, she ran down the hall and into the bathroom, hiding there, waiting for the family experience to be photographed and the first meeting with the first family's dog to end. The Obamas loved it, by the way, and Michelle Obama made certain that Lizet was among the first to see one of Bo's new tricks.

But back to the potato. . . . We're sure you want to know the reason why Lizet had the potato filter on her laptop in the first place. We did too. She was preparing for a meeting with a large group of Latino leaders from across the country, and since the meeting was virtual, she was looking for things she could use as filters to bring lighthearted fun to the group. She recognized that we all need a little bit of laughter in our lives. She aimed for providing this to a group of Latino leaders nationwide and ended up making over forty-five million people laugh and chuckle around the world. She has since been interviewed by the *Today* show in Australia, *HuffPost*, the *Washington Post*, eight different news media outlets in the UK, and us! Her staff even found a way to barter for a potato-embroidered sweatshirt made by one of her fans to present to her for her birthday. People need to laugh. People want to laugh. Thank you, Lizet.

Laugh Hero #2

So, it would be fair to ask, Do I have to turn myself into vegetation to make my staff know that I can have a good time, laugh at myself, not take myself so seriously, and have fun? The answer is no. There are other examples of leaders being themselves, real human beings, and still allowing for laughter and fun in the workplace.

Imagine a very, very large organization, doing vital work that impacts health care for millions. The stress levels are real and at times quite intense. Now, envision your leader's boss as, let's say, demanding in ways that make your teammates cringe. He believes that he is making the difference, has foresight like no other, is transforming the organization like no one else could, and possesses intellectual capacity beyond reproach! Don't get us wrong. A nice enough guy, but whiny, requiring relentless attention, and demanding emotional and professional validation pretty much around the clock. Sort of like a toddler.

The leader of the team serving this needy boss asks her staff one morning, "Hey, did you all get a chance to review that report yet? Diaper boy is waiting, and you know how he gets when he doesn't get what he wants." You read that right. Diaper boy (DB). And it still makes everyone laugh.

Who actually came up with the nickname DB is still a mystery. It wasn't meant in a disrespectful way. The team actually enjoyed their boss, who, to be fair, was quite the visionary and intelligent man. Just a teensy, tiny bit needy, shall we say? Just enough to warrant a few eye rolls across the room. And given the pressure that his team operated under 24/7, coining a nickname was nothing more than a subtle "We love him, but he drives us crazy" gesture.

For her part, the team leader understood. Her team was not insolent in any way. They were hardworking and committed. Her decision was to chuckle, understand, and be a part of the lighthearted fun, which was offered with love, helping everyone cope with the stressors they were experiencing. It endeared her to the team. She wasn't just their boss, she was a real human part of the team. This leader, who walked the fine line between a hard-charging and talented staff and DB, was Raquel "Rocky" Bono, a vice admiral in the Navy (uh, that's three stars for anyone who is counting, and one of only eleven women in the history of the Navy to reach this rank).

To say that Rocky Bono, a woman whose Filipino parents maintained a no-excuses environment, is extremely successful would be an understatement of extraordinary magnitude. She is a trauma surgeon by profession, who served in both Operation Desert Shield and Operation Desert Storm; held a number of senior positions in health care policy; served as a commanding officer; and, prior to her recent retirement, was director of the Defense Health Agency, overseeing the entire military health system. She is currently working with the State of Washington combating the COVID-19 pandemic.

Rocky mastered the art of doing subtle but funny things for her team that let them know she understood. Once when they were stressed by external forces beyond their control, they described to her a feeling of being circled by predators just looking to swoop in and cause problems. Rocky bought all her staff members rubber toy sharks. She gave them out to each member with a message saying that she got it, they were all in it together, and, most important, it was all going to be OK. One of her team members put a ribbon through the fin and still hangs it on her Christmas tree every year, to remind her of the great fun she had with Rocky and her team.

The human connection was never lost on Rocky, and though she held her staff to the highest standards of performance, she knew when to be supportive. On one occasion, one of her staff members was taking a new admiral to her very first meeting. The whole team was excited for this first chance to make their team shine in the eyes of the new boss. And that's about all there is to this story that was good! Rocky's staff member drove the admiral across town to the meeting, delivered her to the location, and waited patiently in the car for her to return. The staffer settled in and checked his BlackBerry for messages (yes, this is an old story). Less than five minutes later, the admiral walked out of the building, sat down in the car, and didn't say a word. The staff member asked, "Meeting is already over?" The admiral said, "No, there never was a meeting, it's next week." Oops.

The staffer, embarrassed and apologetic, reported to Rocky what had happened. Rocky convened her team, and after getting all of the details and agreeing on a new process, she said with a smile, "Well, there's nowhere else to go but up from here!" Yes, this was a performance issue with her team, but not really. At this point, it was about feeling safe and cared for. She knew this wasn't a career-ender, and it was certainly far from the life-and-death decisions she faced in the Gulf War. To this day, the driver of that vehicle considers Rocky to be the finest leader he has ever seen.

The word *excellence* describes how Rocky, now retired from active duty, lived and practiced, whether it was in surgery, brushing her teeth, or interacting with people on a day-to-day basis. The beauty of Rocky is that she maintained superiority in everything she did, but she never discounted the human side of leading people. She held herself and her team accountable for performance, lovingly and laughingly. She allowed herself to have fun with her team and be a part of it, even while leading complicated missions. Her life's passion to create one of the finest health care systems in the world was the driver for actions and decisions, and she did so with a focus on people, on healing, and on humanity. She had fun along the way, even doing a video with Elmo from *Sesame Street*, but that's for another book!

What We Learn from Lizet and Rocky

Lizet and Rocky are pretty funny, we're just sayin'. But not so much in a ha-ha way. They are masterful at the unexpected. They both built careers based on professional expertise and the willingness to hold people accountable. They were well-liked by their peers and were professionally competent. Humorous was not likely how people in their spheres would have described them prior to working with them. But once one got to know them, watch out!

Rocky may seem larger-than-life to some. Since she was one of the very few female vice admirals in the Navy, one could easily get lost in her impressive list of accomplishments. To our knowledge, she doesn't own a copy of the book Philogelos (y'all remember that, don't you? Please tell us yes! Chapter 4). For that matter, nor does Lizet. Neither one quotes books, special programs, or the latest marketable approaches to leadership. They believe in those they lead and have led. They also own their past.

Rocky is a strong believer in her father's philosophy that people must "meet or exceed," and she applied those standards to everyone she led. Lives were at stake. But Rocky was skillful at being able to balance this extraordinary burden with her need to lead people. The message was, This is serious, and we need 100 percent commitment. But . . . Rocky knew that going overboard would dampen the team's innovation and ultimately wear them down. It would prevent her team from accomplishing their mission. Innocent nicknames, sharks, and a little levity and fun made Rocky human to her team members.

Lizet also finds strong roots in her hardworking immigrant parents and carried those admirable values into her career. Growing up with a mother and father who worried about food armed Lizet with a life perspective that very few of us can imagine. It allowed her to keep things in perspective. When interrupting the first family's Kodak moment, she was able to settle on a perspective that mistakes happen, people laugh, and human beings need to find joy in unexpected places, like the private residence of the White House.

Perhaps one of the most impressive things about Lizet and Rocky is their ability to rely on their real, human selves instead of a prescribed regimen of comedy. A common mistake by leaders attempting to use humor in the workplace is scripting their approach. It's understandable and forgivable, but it still doesn't work. Humor comes from the heart and the soul. It's embedded in who we are as people, with all of our faults and scars. Self-deprecating humor, like a potato filter, has an essence of innocence and purity. It allows us to connect.

Both of these extraordinary leaders also found and probably continue to find comfort in allowing humor to be situational. Indeed, a little lighthearted comedic banter can occur at any time during the workday. Zoom meetings, presentations, end-of-year budget analyses, and strategic planning sessions are typically pretty boring and come with a wide array of possibilities for a clever quip. Neither Lizet nor Rocky missed these opportunities. Knowing the benefit of a relaxed and engaged workplace, and not being too wrapped up with their own bad selves, Lizet and Rocky slipped humor in whenever they could.

Finally, just let go. This is what Rocky and Lizet did so well. Despite childhood trials, professional accomplishments, and current workplace challenges, they allowed humor to be present. Neither took herself too seriously, even when times were serious. They both had decisions to make. They could be on guard, wearing their mask, or they could release their inner being, their real self. By letting go, they also made it real with their teams. And who wouldn't want to work for either of these two phenomenal leaders?

CHAPTER 6

THE LAUGHTER BEHAVIORS

We promised that we would be completely honest as we were writing this book. Our goal was to write something from our hearts to yours, supported by research and delivered in a simple and understandable format. Unlike when we wrote the part of the book preceding love behaviors, your authors did not have a spirited discussion here! But we do have the same concerns.

As with love, one can't certify oneself in laughter. One of our biggest fears is that you may read this chapter and attempt to become the office prankster. This would be a huge mistake. Comedy cannot be taught. And humble, self-effacing humor must come from the heart. It is not something you can create by simply reading joke books or watching stand-up comedy. You can't take a course, and if you do, it will be a waste of your money. A comfort with laughter begins by you being you, as so many things do. Knowing yourself and how humor fits in your life outside of work is a good place to start.

Now, about those THREE BIG THINGS that we can't stand presenting but we know we must. There's certainly no shortage of views as to what is necessary in order to exercise the use of humor effectively in leadership. Well, compared with love, it's a little sparse, but the research is still there. It is our humble opinion that the secrets of the use of laughter in leadership are connected to each of us on a very personal level. Comfort and awareness of self is the foundation of being able to laugh at oneself and with others. In many ways, we are at our most vulnerable when we are laughing.

What we present below, as in the chapter on love, is a conscious choice for you. These choices can be a struggle, and at least two of the three come with risks. They require the self-awareness for which we made our earlier case, and they necessitate an effort on our part to be extremely sensitive to others. Only then will laughter and humor yield the benefits to leadership that we espouse.

Your Laughter Choices

Courage

Courage in the workplace has certainly been a much-discussed topic over the years. A lot has been written about courage in leadership, and frankly, we agree—it takes fortitude to step into a leadership role. Often, it is a foray into the unknown. Exciting? It can be. Intriguing? Perhaps. Frightening? It better be! Leadership comes with risk. If done properly, leading entails a lot of *putting it out there*, both professionally and personally.

Professionally, new leaders are expected to introduce something completely different. They transcend their previous comfort levels with their technical expertise and, let's be honest, their success to assume new risks—the risks of leading others. When you think of all the emotional baggage that we carry as human beings, leading others is a formidable task indeed. Workers are not simple cogs in the wheel. They are thinking and feeling human beings who have needs far beyond their job descriptions.

Personally, the leadership pathway can be taxing as well. As we step away from previous jobs and tasks with which we are familiar, we move into a world seemingly incomprehensible. Many is the time that a new leader, struggling to find his way in his new role, cradles his head in his hands and proclaims, "I have no idea how to handle this! My kingdom for a nonsupervisory position!"

It's going to be OK. Just takes a little courage!

When we think of courage, we rightly think of people who took great personal risk. Martin Luther King Jr. Anne Frank. Or, more recently, Danica Roem, who unseated a twenty-six-year incumbent in 2017 to become the first openly transgender person to serve in the Virginia House of Delegates. There's also Lieutenant Colonel Alexander Vindman, a key witness in the Trump impeachment hearings in 2019, who lost his position on the National Security Council as a result of his steadfast courage.

Author Bill Treasurer suggests that courage is the primary virtue of organizational performance. Between the need for sound decision-making and the necessity for creativity and risk tasking, courage often takes center stage in our leadership journey. As part of his research on the topic, Treasurer often distinguishes between three different types of courage: the courage to try, the courage to trust, and the courage to tell (Treasurer 2019).

The courage to try is what allows leaders to stray from their comfort zone. When leaders are able to take steps that they have not taken before, even those that require some risk, they are exerting the courage to try. They are willing to assume responsibilities for previously incomplete initiatives that others may have begun and not finished. These leaders are willing to take a chance at something new and untested, efforts that may be considered groundbreaking. They keep going.

The courage to trust is the *letting go* courage, and it is one of the more difficult of the three. As leaders move into new roles and assume new challenges, they are often expected to leave previous responsibilities in the past. This can feel like a loss of self or loss of control, but it is crucial to trust those who follow in their path. The courage to trust requires that leaders assume noble intent on the part of all with whom they work. When leaders let go and allow others to step into their shoes, or when they readily delegate the work of an important project, they are exhibiting the courage to trust.

The courage to tell is the courage that allows leaders to think independently and speak candidly. It requires all of the components of love that we wrote about in chapter 3—self-awareness, vulnerability, and kindness. Those with the courage to tell are in touch with their feelings and aware of their inner signals. They communicate openly and honestly and are able to offer their message in a way that exudes forthrightness. Leaders with the courage to tell are also able to admit mistakes and utter the words we rarely hear in professional settings: "I'm sorry."

There is a fourth type of courage that we'd like to toss out there, the courage to chill. Yes, you read that correctly, the courage to chill. This is no slight on any person or anyone's job, but we do often take ourselves and our positions too seriously, and this is a massive barrier to our ability to lead and connect with others. This *serious factor* hampers our ability to enjoy our lives, to learn, to have fun, to be creative, and, yes, to laugh. Maybe we have a lot to learn from Paraguay. It is consistently ranked as the most chill country in the world.

Admittedly, life is tough. Work is challenging. But without the courage to chill, we fall into the trap of living in a constant state of fear. We fear ridicule. We fear not being good enough. We fear shame. We fear failure. We live, unfailingly, looking over our shoulder and double-checking our thoughts, words, and deeds. We are in a state of consistent self-loathing and fear of rejection.

What's worse, we tend to view others with the same level of gravity, and that's not fun for anyone. It creates a work environment of stress and anxiety. People and production suffer. We make poor decisions.

Having the courage to chill begins with giving yourself a break. Trust us, no one can live up to the expectations that you set for yourself. Why create a new set of unrealistic expectations? The power of personal forgiveness is an extraordinary force. When we adjust our own expectations of self, we create a new playing field, one that is more level and more forgiving.

Looking at life differently also goes a long way in building the courage to chill. This requires the fourth-person perspective that we discussed in chapter 3. Build your chill factor by looking at yourself looking at situations. What fears do you have, what concerns, and what baggage? Sometimes simply writing a list of the things that are weighing you down can be a very powerful practice for addressing them directly. You are then free to find the positives in yourself, others, and your life. And while we're on that subject, one of the authors says that Barry Manilow was right (and he's always right). It can be daybreak if we want to believe. Finding the positive will reframe the way you see the world. A smile is soon to follow.

Courage comes in all forms. It may be emotional, physical, spiritual, or moral. And far from the historical views of courage (tough, strong, powerful, commanding), the leader of today exhibits courage in subtler ways, and they're more human. Courage today is about letting go and being real. It's about unleashing that human being inside of us that we hide behind whether it be the title we carry or the office we hold. Today's courage brings teams together and fires up the hearts of those we lead. It is uniting, not dividing. It's about the soft touch, not a stern voice. It's chill.

Finally, recall that this book is about love and laughter, and it may surprise you to know that the original Latin root for the word *courage* is *cor*. *Cor* is the Latin word for "heart." Heart is a symbol for love, and love is in the title of the book. See how this all ties together?

Hmmm. . . . ☺

Humility

Humility suffers from the opposite problem as courage. Commonly, the big bad leaders who make the headlines for their aggressive tone and bigger-than-life stature quickly get tagged with the label of courage. They're risk takers! They plow through the workforce insisting on loyalty, productivity, and commitment. They destroy the competition with risky new ventures. They don't inspire as much as they command. They have really, really starched shirts and blouses. But these leaders aren't necessarily courageous (even when they speak in deep, gravelly tones), and they rarely carry the reputation of humility.

From a very early age, we are taught to advertise our talents. The simple processes involved in primary and secondary education lend themselves to measurement of one's knowledge accumulation. We're graded. We're ranked. And the poor millennials got the worst of it. They are the most measured and observed generation ever. Toss in social media, where we are encouraged by friends, family, and society to put forth the perfect image of ourselves and our lives, and one can see where humility might take a back seat. One might also see why letting go and being real might be a hard choice to make.

There's an artificiality to a workplace without humility. Who we are is not what we accomplish, or the grades we earn, or the degrees. Somewhere our true self gets lost in our need to showcase our talents or nudge a coworker aside to take credit. We posture and preen. We seek to be seen by the right people at the right time. Taken to the extreme, this translates into a workplace of distrust and nonconstructive competitiveness. We become just another tool for achieving organizational metrics. Lost are the individual, the joy, the fun.

Probably the most powerful voice where humility is concerned, at least initially, is that of Jim Collins. It's hard to believe that it's been over twenty years since the publication of his groundbreaking book, *Good to Great: Why Some Companies Make the Leap . . . and Others Don't*, which many consider one of the best management books of all time. The result of Collins's five years of research identified the key factors present in organizations that transcended being simply good companies to becoming great companies. There were two. First, the leaders had a sense of fierce resolve, a commitment and drive toward success. Second was the element that all of these leaders shared: humility.

Thank you, Jim.

We're afraid there are still too many who question the value of humility. The chorus of objectors point to the need to have a big ego so that people will have someone to follow. They suggest a disconnect between staff and leaders who don't put themselves in the spotlight. Oh, the research is there, such as it is, but it isn't convincing. There will always be egos that succeed. Many, many more fail.

Others propose that humility is weak. Humble people lack self-esteem and confidence. They don't have the ability to defend their ideas, if they have any at all. In the workplace, these passive beings are run over by the more aggressive voices in the boardroom. They don't stand up for themselves, so they won't stand up for others. They seem to blend into the furnishings like coffee creamer. Frankly, those making this proposal don't really understand what humility means or looks like.

The facts are that research, and lots of it, suggests the opposite. In the last twenty or so years, multiple studies have shown the unquestioned benefits of humility in leadership. Leaders who are humble cast a wide net of connection across those whom they lead, setting the stage for richer organizational cultures and for better engagement, trust, and performance. Younger generations, especially, are requiring humility as a core value in their leadership and their companies.

In a study published in the *Journal of Management*, researchers sought to determine whether or not humble leaders had an impact on organizational performance and internal processes. Their findings, along with the research of many others, show that humility in the top echelon of organizational leadership is directly correlated to improved performance, teamwork, decision-making processes, vision creation, and information sharing (Ou, Waldman, and Peterson 2018).

The work of Pepperdine University psychologist Elizabeth J. Krumrei-Mancuso paints an even more convincing picture of the value of humility. Krumrei-Mancuso distinguished a unique type of humility—intellectual humility, a sensitivity to the fallibility of our views on social and political matters. Given the divisiveness in our nation, the timing couldn't be better! She initially found that intellectual humility was unrelated to IQ or political affiliation. Humility can exist anywhere. The bulk of her results suggest that humility is a predictor of curiosity, open-mindedness, empathy, gratitude, altruism, and benevolence. Not bad attributes for today's leaders, we're just sayin'. People with higher levels of intellectual humility were also less apt to dig in their heels on their beliefs and respected the views of others. They were also less likely to be interested in accumulating workplace power (Krumrei-Mancuso 2017). Humility allows for that openness and space to be real.

Importantly, leaders need to understand that you can't fake it until you make it. The same applies to humility. In one study, researchers made a direct connection between employees' perception of a leader's level of humility and the employees' willingness to engage (Yang, Zhang, and Chen 2019). Employees who perceived their leader as being authentically humble, and not doing so for some faux corporate initiative, were more committed. Most important, they trusted the leader more. So, if we're going to be humble, we'd better mean it.

It's not that difficult to see humility in leaders. They are sincere and modest. They are able to laugh at themselves openly and find humor in the day-to-day trials they face. Humble leaders make you feel at home and welcome. Much like Rocky and Lizet, they are unpretentious, despite their success. They know they stand on the shoulders of those who came before them, and all they seek is to make a positive difference. This isn't difficult for them, because they excel at fostering teamwork and collaboration. They understand that organizational success is tied to far more than their talents. They're confident but not arrogant. They can let go and have fun.

Humble leaders are not perfect, and they know it. When they make mistakes, they admit it. They own their shortcomings but are not bound by them and will sometimes even joke about them. They are unabashed learners and look for every opportunity to continue to grow as leaders and people. Humble leaders are gracious and noble while on their developmental path. They seek, constantly. And since they are so comfortable with who they are, they can laugh a little.

Are there downsides to humility? We think not. Some suggest that overly humble people fail to take advantage of competitive opportunities or they don't market themselves enough. They don't take center stage enough to be noticed by superiors or respected by subordinates. But we don't buy it. Aptitude speaks louder than showboating. Too often, grandstanding is used by the weak in lieu of talent.

People see through this. Authentic humble leaders will always gain the trust and commitment of those they lead far more readily than the performer or the narcissistic egomaniac. Humility will always win.

Social Awareness

It's the simple act of noticing. Geez, we wish we could remember who said that! It's a wildly popular phrase on the internet for anything related to mindfulness or meditation, but we heard this from one of our colleagues some years back. It's such a poignant and powerful phrase—or better yet, a challenge. It is the simple act of noticing that underpins social awareness. Remember that bringing humor and laughter into the workplace requires social and cultural awareness.

Like courage, social awareness has received much attention in recent years. Once we've succeeded in the very difficult effort of building self-awareness and developing self-management skills, we are ready to turn our attention to our surroundings. How do others look to us? What are their unique cultural and personal needs? What about organizations? Got politics? While all of these fall under the social awareness umbrella, most researchers suggest that social awareness involves three critical components: organizational awareness, service, and empathy.

A lack of organizational awareness may be one of the most common barriers that leaders face. Leaders often assume new roles and immediately begin making their mark by shifting reporting structures and creating new organizational charts so that they can make immediate change. Simple organizational awareness with a focus on the informal relationships, politics, and culture would suggest caution in such a situation. Organizations of human beings are living, breathing organisms with hearts and souls. They have good days and bad days. They have jeans that don't fit on some days. Organizationally aware leaders observe much in the same way that a maestro would conduct a symphony, watching the entire organization, being aware of how it works together, and making subtle adjustments.

The service aspect of social awareness is the capacity to recognize and meet the needs of outside clients. This may sound simple enough, but when we become too focused on internal operations or personal gratification, the very consumers who depend on us move elsewhere. This service aspect also extends to a service ethic. How do we serve those whom we lead? How hard do we work to keep our customers happy? How hard do we work to keep our employees happy? As an organization, do we go the extra mile with personalized or customized service to create a memorable experience for our employees? Do we make them laugh?

We saved the best and most important component of social awareness for last: empathy. Certainly, understanding our organizations, customer bases, and employee experiences matters, but empathy is the quality that calls us to connect with others. It is the ability to recognize and appreciate the emotions and viewpoints of other people. It is a thoughtful and considerate practice whereby we place our own needs aside and focus on comfort and understanding. We dig deep inside ourselves to find something in our past that allows us to relate to another person, to feel what he or she feels. This is when we can truly understand what might be OK to laugh about or when it might just be OK to share a funny moment. Empathy is a powerful combination of self-awareness, self-management, and vulnerability, and it is unmatched in its power to bridge.

Just a side note about empathy. Sadly, we appear to be in an empathy deficit in our country, and empathy has been on the decline for many years. College students report being less concerned about empathetic behaviors and more comfortable with a more self-centered approach. Research by Sara Konrath found that there may be many reasons, and all of them are tied to fewer connections with other people (Konrath et al. 2010). People are less likely to join community groups or sports teams. Social media makes it easy to "unfriend" with the click of a button. Sadly, the recent isolation caused by the COVID-19 pandemic is almost certain to have a similar impact, since living with interaction via computer screen is a far cry from real human contact.

Unlike courage and humility, social awareness has a special place in the humor discussion because of comedy's potential to offend. Leaders must take exceptional care to understand their audiences so as to benefit from the advantages of humor. Part of this challenge lies in recognizing that not all people will find a funny comment entertaining. Even in a room where everyone is laughing, there are degrees of funny that span a wide scale. Some are losing their breath because they are laughing so hard, while others are managing a polite and stoic smile.

There are now five generations actively employed in the workplace, and this is, indeed, where the disparity in laughs will most likely appear. Experts note that at a younger age, we tend to find more things funny because of the novelty of our surroundings. As adults, we have a long history of experiences and perspectives that color our views on humor. Cultural ties play a role as well. What's funny to an American may be vastly different from what amuses someone from India. Generation Zs speak a different language than Boomers, so gaps in humor there may be present as well.

Still, with a little practice, we can hone the social awareness skills needed to make the workplace more accepting and a little funnier. Listening is a good place to start. Dan Goleman once described poor listening as the common cold of leadership. "*Sorry, Dan, we weren't listening—what did you say?*" It is true, though, that subpar listening skills are common, and the impact on those we don't listen to is significant. When we fidget, look at our phone, or multitask while someone is speaking to us, we are sending a strong message of disinterest. Instead of listening actively and empathetically, we tend to spend that time formulating our response. A deep breath and a little patience go a long way in helping to improve poor listening skills.

Leaders with strong social awareness also pick up on nonverbal cues, which is a great skill to have when trying out humor. While it's a bit of an overstatement to say that anyone who crosses their arms is closing themselves off, it's not too much to suggest that nonverbals matter. Macro- and microaggressions send strong messages, as do facial expressions. Lifting of the eyebrows or movement of one or both corners of the lips can send signals ranging from humble inquiry to tacit disapproval. Posture and gestures such as waving and pointing are also clues to engagement.

Finally, it is important to note that social awareness, since it is based in observation, is undeniably about patience. Patience is indeed a virtue, but it's not a common virtue among many of us. The day-to-day pace of life and work for most of us leaves little time for patience. Couple this with a society based largely on instant gratification, and it's no wonder that we lose it when our Starbucks order takes too long. Leaders who are patient arm themselves with the time they need to observe. They are able to see things in others, their employees, and their organizations that provide clues as to what is really going on. This paves the way for more enriched dialogue that builds self-esteem, bonds across the enterprise, and allows for that much-needed laughter.

Organizational Impact of Laughter

Think of the times when you, as a customer, sought a service and were treated to a little fun along the way. No one in the world makes boarding an aircraft more fun than Southwest Airlines. Their in-flight announcements are funny too—like the time when a flight attendant, at twenty thousand feet, reminded everyone that the smoking area was outside at the end of the starboard wing. Some of the funniest insurance commercials come from Geico. And what about the brilliant Head & Shoulders commercial featuring memorable banter between NFL stars Patrick Mahomes and Troy Polamalu? Think these organizations have had success? And consider Rocky and Lizet. Think they've been successful? Made a difference?

Humor matters. A 2012 study from the *Journal of Managerial Psychology* revealed a comprehensive listing of organizational benefits of workplace humor, including improved performance, enhanced employee satisfaction, better workgroup cohesion, healthier employees, less burnout, and reduced stress (Mesmer-Magnus et al. 2012).

And if you're still not listening, stop being a grump. It isn't like employees don't want this. Everyone likes a good chuckle. We start at three months old with peekaboo and go from there. OK, your authors aren't advocating this game, but let's be honest, wouldn't it be a trip to start a meeting with a round of musical chairs? Maybe we are advocating after all! But the bottom line is, when your team is having fun, they are happier and more productive. They're relaxed, which leads to more innovation and creativity. Isn't that worth it? And there's more . . .

- **It improves your reputation.** Want to improve how you're viewed in an organization? Researchers found that when someone tells an appropriate joke, he is automatically perceived as more competent in both new and existing relationships. He is also viewed as having a higher organizational status. Turns out that humor is a critical mediator in how individuals view one another hierarchically and in groups (Bitterly et al. 2017).
- **Laughter in the workplace makes the workforce healthier.** Research continues to support the notion that laughter has serious physiological benefits, including chemical changes in the body that reduce stress (Louie et al. 2016). A low-stress workplace yields fewer sick days, a healthier environment, and a more cohesive workforce.
- **Laughter brings us together.** Laughter may be a collective social behavior, but does it draw us closer together? Uh, the answer is yeah! Researchers have uncovered how laughter connects us in a unique and measurable way (Kurtz and Algoe 2017). This promotes stronger social bonds in and out of the workplace. Remember, the majority of our laughter is not at jokes, it's simply tied to being in the company of others.
- **Laughter improves productivity.** A University of Bristol study found a well-kept secret to employee productivity: watch a comedy show. After doing as much, employees were 10

percent more productive (Proto 2016). And leave it to those Australians again. In an article published in the *Journal of Business and Psychology*, researchers found that humor can increase persistence on individual tasks (Cheng and Wang 2014).

- **Yes, Virginia, laughter makes us more creative.** When we are able to laugh in the workplace, our brains overdose on creativity. When we feel connection with others in a way that frees us from fear and judgment, we are far more likely to explore previously uncharted pathways of thought.
- **Humor is a motivator.** A little occasional silliness is a huge morale booster. In today's workforce, one immersed in competition and pressure, humor can lighten the load immensely. And since we know that we tend to laugh in groups more heartily than alone, why the heck not? Crack a joke and let's get this party started.
- **Humor starts a meeting like nothing else can.** It may be one of the most familiar and most uncomfortable moments we endure—the quiet and discomforting moment sitting around a table awaiting the start of yet another dreaded meeting. Perhaps a quick quip about how no one is wearing green or how "excited" we all are to be in another meeting will do the trick, or "This gathering reminds me of an awkward dinner with my in-laws . . ." Anything to start the flow!
- **It humans you.** OK, *human* is not a verb, but we're using it as one here. Humor is the ultimate bridge builder. The psychosocial dynamic, along with verbal and nonverbal cues, can connect even the most disparate team members. Senior executives and front-line workers join together in a moment of pure enjoyment. What's not to love?

We can tell you're hooked. You're willing and ready to exert the courage, reveal the humility, and be sensitive to others in your attempt to bring humor to bear. Good for you. But not so fast. The number of people who try to use humor effectively and fail is staggering. They often make the rookie mistakes of telling off-color jokes or feeling like they have to do something really off the wall, like wearing silly clothes. Other leaders err significantly through the use of "Just kidding" after an inappropriate comment. In her book *The Fearless Organization: Creating Psychological Safety in the Workplace for Learning, Innovation, and Growth*, author and professor Amy Edmondson describes the phenomenon and notes that when "Just kidding" follows an inappropriate comment, it is likely that the speaker knew deep down that what he or she said was unsuitable (Edmondson 2019). Reserved and introverted leaders may struggle with exactly how to express a lighter, more carefree vibe and may be prone to these mistakes, albeit innocently. Beware of these errors. They impair your professional reputation. Further, they're inauthentic performances that will bore at best and offend at worst.

We left out one very important detail—the dark side. We mentioned before that humor, unlike love, can be a double-edged sword. It has the capacity to bridge and the capacity to divide. It can bring people together in raucous laughter, and it can offend to tears. Andrew Tarvin, in his book *Humor That Works: The Missing Skill for Success and Happiness at Work*, describes humor as a screwdriver, useful but involving a twist. The right technique and the right tool can yield positives. But if humor distracts, divides, or disparages, it can yield nightmares (Tarvin 2019). Those who use humor for these purposes cause organizational and personal damage. So it goes that the use of humor comes with responsibility. Extraordinary responsibility.

As we mentioned earlier, the use of humor brings challenges that love does not. Humor is contextual, and that makes its use tricky indeed, especially where self-deprecation or sarcasm is concerned. In their superb article "Sarcasm, Self-Deprecation, and Inside Jokes: A User's Guide to Humor at Work," Brad Bitterly and Alison Wood Brooks offer a compelling outline of how and when to use humor.

Bitterly and Brooks see value in the sarcastic approach when leaders are trying to enhance innovation. Importantly, though, use sarcasm only with those you know and trust. Sarcasm can be risky outside a familiar crowd and can be misconstrued when the leader is attempting to build trust or new relationships. Self-deprecation works if one is poking fun at an unimportant personal characteristic but can backfire if one is referring to something more substantive with an audience who has yet to see one as competent. Finally, inside jokes can be successful if, when making the comment, you ensure that no one is left out. If someone isn't in on the joke, it's not inside humor (Bitterly and Brooks 2020). Know your audience!

When used properly, the timing of humor matters, whether it be in a hallway conversation or in a meeting. The audience matters as well. It goes without saying that frivolity among colleagues is the easiest path. Generally, peers are more welcoming of informality and often welcome the camaraderie and bonding. But it's important to note that humor can be effective up and down the chain of authority. Using humor with those for whom we work is one of the most effective ways of putting them at ease. Who doesn't want a relaxed boss who doesn't take herself too seriously?

We leave you with this: for our money, the safest approach to humor in leadership is the self-deprecating joke, the one-liner that brings you to the same level as those around you, the one that provides the bridge. A brief joke at one's own expense says you're human. It says you don't fall into the previously described trap of taking yourself too seriously. And if the joke fails, who cares? You'll still be viewed as smarter. Don't underestimate the power of this approach. When it's done appropriately and authentically, with a wink and a smile, the results can be impactful.

So, Try This

- Observe closely and count the number of times you hear laughter in the workplace in a given day.

- Ask your team to gauge your chill factor on a scale of one to ten (ten being in the super-chill Beatles music category). Think about what the results tell you.
- What was the last funny thing you said or did in the workplace? Was it in front of a group or in the safer confines of your office with only a handful of people? When was the last time you laughed while at work? Try it, if you haven't.

And Finally

Those who subscribe to strict, turgid work environments with no humor are fashioning organizations with little chance for real creativity, along with teams far more prone to utilizing excessive amounts of sick leave, job burnout, and turnover. Laughter in the workplace is the perfect antidote to workforces infected with the diseases of pride, competition, and distrust.

It's not easy to let go and laugh, but it is possible. Lizet did it; so did Rocky. And they both made huge impacts on their organizations. Their willingness to embrace the authenticity that comes with a sense of humor literally casts a light over those whose lives they touch. What more could we want in our leaders?

PART III

THE LEAP

CHAPTER 7

YOU HAVE PERMISSION—NOW WHAT?

Not really. Well, not that you really needed our permission. Maybe it would be best to say that you now have our wish for you, our plea. Love and laughter is where it's at for leadership, and we don't want that message to get lost. And as much as we hope you've enjoyed the book so far, we strongly suspect there's a number of you out there who may have some doubts. Perish the thought!

Despite the fact that we have peppered the book with valid scientific data, love, and more humor than the average reader can stand, we also recognize that at this point in the book you've been exposed to so much feel-good information, your mind might be in sensory overload. At best you may be thinking, "Yeah, finally! These guys got it right! This does matter more than anything else!" For this reader, your autographed copy of the book is in the mail.

The "OK, So Wait a Minute (OSWAM)" Leader

Others may have a different take. We call them the "OK, so wait a minute" leaders. After "OK, so wait a minute," they follow with anything from "I got this already" to "It won't work in my organization" to "I can't do this." Good! Your feelings are valid, and your concerns are real. As leaders ourselves, we've struggled to let go and get real.

It's risky. But check this out—all those other approaches, theories, graphics, reports, and pathways to leadership don't work without this first. So maybe you've stumbled onto the right approach. Just maybe! The fact that you're still with us gives us the chance to change your mind. Will you let us try?

The final chapter of this book is all about showing you the path to embrace love and laughter in your life as a way of being, not just a way of leading. The concerns about this being just another happy book are legitimate, so we're going to steer away from offering the traditional leadership recipe of "Be kind, engage, communicate, etc." Instead, we are embracing the pessimism to this approach. So, let's talk about these concerns and how we might maneuver your heart and soul in a way to open your sense of self and who you really are. If we get there, you're on the brink of living a life with love and laughter, discovering your mindset, and embracing core human needs that we all share.

OSWAM—"I Got This!"

Meet Leon, an executive with more than twenty-five years of experience in his profession. When he started moving up in his organization, he was noticed by senior leadership as an up-and-comer because of his astute technical knowledge. His work was always timely, he stayed within budget, and he got along pretty well with his team members, as long as they didn't question his expertise. No one ever outwardly complained about working with Leon, so his bosses gave him opportunities to lead project teams, which, though not earth-shattering, by and large were successful. After attending a few mandatory leadership development programs, Leon had earned his stripes and was given a role as a department head.

One day, Leon learned that he was getting a new boss, Kamille. Kamille showed a lot of interest in Leon and his success in the organization. They met several times and discussed his team, goals, projects, and plan for moving forward. But all was not well. The more Kamille got to know Leon, the more she started picking up on

Leon's language and use of leadership jargon such as "I'm an authentic leader who uses design thinking with integrity" and "I am also a change agent, well versed in emotional intelligence. I always ask my team how they are doing on a regular basis." Kamille found herself hearing the same canned phrases over and over again. It felt like a scorecard.

Upon closer observation, Kamille noticed a few things about Leon. He was often found walking from cubicle to cubicle, greeting his team members, checking in with them. He professed an open-door policy, and in truth his door was always somewhat physically open, but no one ever approached him with feedback or a suggestion. In morning check-ins, his team members would each respond obediently with short, noncontroversial updates and get back to work immediately. The team meetings were all business; structured; on time; and focused on outcomes, next steps, and responsibilities. If anyone had a question, they would ask Leon, he would provide the answer, and they would move on. No complaints, no problems, a clockwork operation, right? Not so much.

Kamille also took notice of the fact that team members did not spend much time with each other in groups, catching up on life and such. Leon would disappear into his office after check-in, door ajar, and get back to work himself. There was no laughter, no connection, no familiarity. When she asked Leon how engaged and happy his team was in their jobs, his response, quite naturally, was that no one was complaining. "I've got this," he would claim. "All is well, no problems." Ah, but there were.

Get out! You're the "I got this" leader? Oh, man! Let us just say, we love ya. We love everyone, but that doesn't mean we love you less. Here's what we know about you: You live in a wonderful make-believe land, but it's a land not of pastels, unicorns, and rainbows, but rather a world of black and white. Simple distinctions. Easy. You have all the answers. You've done this before. If you haven't seen it all, you've seen most of it. So, what's not to love?

Look, everyone brings their share of imperfections to the world of leadership, but we have serious concerns about the "I got this" leader. In fact, it may be one of the primary reasons we wrote this book. Anytime anyone gets comfortable with any specific body of knowledge, whether it be technical, philosophical, operational, or enological, problems arise. And sadly, this leader is all too common (but we still love them).

Those who've had to adjust to working with this leader report similar experiences. Right and wrong. My way or the highway! Got a question? About anything? You've found your leader! Maybe you didn't know this, but they got it! Just prostrate yourself before their throne, and they will give you the divine wisdom of which you seek! And dream someday of being just like them! These leaders don't need teams of talented minds around them. Innovation in the workforce spells the possibility of failure, and that's not something embraced by this leader. They don't need thinkers, they simply need doers—those who will follow them blindly, hanging on every word, and waiting for the next set of divinely inspired instructions.

Leaders in this vein don't mind being asked questions as long as it feeds their need to share their knowledge. They will generally reply with their answer, which may not be the answer, just their answer. Their expectation is that the subordinate will nod dutifully and move on to the next task at hand. Probing questions are the worst for these leaders because they prolong inquiry and run the risk of exposing this leader as not knowing the answer. Exploratory questions, by their nature, invite uncertainty and wonder. They serve as a challenge to the "I got this" leader's knowledge-based authority.

There is also another very impactful problem with these leaders—their inability to see their organization. Take, in the above example, Leon's complete lack of awareness of the environment he's created. His confidence that his people are all good is misplaced and woefully wrong. If there is a need for love in the department that Leon oversees, he's not seeing it. And laughter? Not a chance. Unless it's a quick one-liner that he tosses out at one of his morning meetings (trust us, we know Leon—he doesn't), it's not likely that his environment will be one where any measure of fun will develop. And no surprise, if he cracks a joke, it will be a bad one, and everyone will laugh, just like they are supposed to.

"I Got This!" Barriers to Love and Laughter

"I got this" leaders do not make the space for love and laughter in their workplace because they don't need to. It's not part of their data bank of expertise, and any foray into a softer, complex, emotionally laden universe is one of uncertainty. By maintaining an all-knowing presence, these leaders need not risk straying from their comfort levels. They already know it all, so what else is there? This false bravado could be based on experience, or that expensive course they took at the luxury training center with watered-down vodka and rubber-chicken dinners. No matter the venue, the confidence is now ingrained.

This leads to one of the most substantial obstructions to love and laughter: the struggle of the "I've got this" leader to learn. Strike that. They don't struggle, because they don't try. Many times, this unwillingness to learn is connected to the fragile ego we all carry. A sense of self matters to all of us, and for the all-knowing leader it is the currency of worth. Learning, by definition, means we don't know something. That's kryptonite to a leader who considers himself the font of all knowledge. Becoming a student again is not akin to the roles many of us play: supervisor, manager, parent.

All-knowing leaders may have experienced success—many do—and that's what they rest upon.

Neurologically this make sense. The brain is very comfortable with the knowledge it has already mastered. As human beings, we tend to rely on that knowledge. It gives us a sense of worth and well-being, and a place in the work community. It gets us to where we want to go and allows us to make quick decisions in emergencies. It's when we get comfortable with that knowledge, rely on our past experiences to predict future ones, and shun the likelihood of new ideas that we become the know-it-all leader. But when we open ourselves to new approaches, radical views, and uncertainty, we open the door to innovation.

There could be another problem from which our all-knowing leader suffers: a lack of confidence. Perhaps it came in the form of a missed promotion or plum job assignment. The self-esteem jolt can be deep, and it causes the leader to dig deeper into her reservoir of knowledge as a source of her leadership strength. Sometimes, a lack of confidence can easily slip into flat-out fear. Fear causes our neurological system to go into shutdown mode, focusing only on survival. This makes it highly unlikely that the leader will ever step out of her comfort zone.

Challenging the "I got this" leader is not usually a good idea. On a good day, you might get the dismissive hand that simply shoos you away. But on a bad day, there's a possibility that the reaction might slip into a little nastiness when his "I got this" is confronted. Leaders who are overly focused on self-achievement, are uninterested in interpersonal relationships, and concentrate on their own self-interest have the ability to strategically regulate their behavior to achieve their own goals.

Finally, sometimes know-it-alls are tamer. They may be simply uninformed, lost, or uncomfortable with straying beyond the graphic depiction of leadership they've been taught over the years.

"I Got This!" Embracing Love and Laughter

It's not easy to make the switch from the "I got this" leader and open one's heart to love and laughter. To be fair, it's not a switch, it's a transition. The fact is, we all experience this phase in our leadership lives at some point. We begin our careers with little outside of an entry-level knowledge base about a specific field. We gain more experience and we get promoted, maybe win a few performance awards, and get promoted again. We're on a roll. But we're also locked into a thinking pattern that depends on expertise. We're not being bad, we're simply being safe. This narrow perspective can lead to the "I got this" mentality.

In order to move beyond this limited viewpoint, we have to let go of those preestablished thinking patterns that convinced us how good we are. They're addictive and comforting and without doubt contribute to success, to a point. It's important to recognize and embrace that we're valuable because of who we are, not what we know. There are a lot of smart people out there, so it's basically a wash.

Letting go of our dependence on what we know may be as easy as simply reaching out publicly to let those who work for us know how much we value what they do and the expertise they bring. Collective IQ always outperforms an individual's IQ. You can also challenge your own self by asking your team what they think of your decisions. This, by the way, won't always work. If you are an omnipresent force, you're not likely to get the constructive feedback you seek. One trick is to create your own mini-360 evaluation that has two simple open-ended statements: I like it when Leon ______; I wish Leon would ______. Pass these around, and have your team slip them on your desk when you're not there. You'll be amazed.

Finally, the all-knowing leader is well-advised to take the time to notice what's around her. In the midst of her "Everything is fine here" perspective, things may be falling apart. Do people stop talking when you walk in the room? Are all of your decisions met with flattering approval from your team? All of them? Give us a break—no one is that good! There's your first clue, so pay attention. Dynamics may not be visible except to the most astute observer. It could be the slightest nonverbal clue from a team member that suggests the need for some compassion, some empathy, or a little joke.

Believe us when we say that we are all imperfect souls, and all of us have strayed through this all-knowing minefield at some point in our careers. In the extreme version of these leaders, they make many miserable and leave trails of bodies on their road to achievement. In a tamer version, they are less damaging in general but still stifling, and they are woefully unaware of how beautiful the workplace can truly become. All because they know it all. They are happy to continue in their prescribed path, comfortable as is and hesitant to change. But when "I got this" leaders take a step away from their expert selves, they open the door to the real possibility of love and laughter.

P.S. By the way—with our love of Malbec, enological issues are bound to come up! ☺

OSWAM—"This Won't Work!"

Meet Jocelyn, a seasoned and well-respected leader in charge of three large program areas in an influential global organization that has been around for many years. The enterprise is a stable and well-respected entity, albeit somewhat bureaucratic. The formal reporting avenues are rigid, and while people in the company accomplish their mission, the workplace is devoid of any vibe beyond getting the work done and leaving as quickly as possible.

Jocelyn, having recently read a magnificent book by Zina and Patrick, wants to see change. It's not something that's happened much in her tenure. She wants to infuse the organization with some levity and a little compassion. She has been observing the people around her, and she's less than enthused about the possibility that she'll be successful. She suspects that reaching out to colleagues and team members for anything other than work requirements would result in blank stares. Even a simple discussion of weekend plans and family vacations is out of the norm. Seeking out opportunities to build relationships with each of her subordinates, eating lunch with them, sharing her own personal stories, making herself as real as possible, would result in a loss of respect and an accusation of crossing the line of professionalism, being too friendly or even intrusive.

Her senior leadership is no help. They refuse to be burdened by "soft" skills they see as unnecessary emotional engagement that won't improve daily operations. They are unfazed by the fact that team members pretty much wear headphones while in their cubicles and barely look up when anyone walks by. As long as the work is getting done, why not leave well enough alone?

If Jocelyn attempted any changes to the status quo, she would be interrupting their work, their progress, and their daily routines.

If she tried to connect with her colleagues outside of the usual work-related topics, she would hear crickets . . . or the sounds of silence (thanks, Simon and Garfunkel!).

Jocelyn wants a love-and-laughter change. She wants to try to connect with her team. She wishes she could help her bosses see the advantages of love and laughter in the workplace. She even purchased a copy of Zina and Patrick's book and left it in her immediate supervisor's office. Last time she looked, he had used it as a coaster. What makes it more difficult is that Jocelyn has many friends and loved ones in her personal life, but when she walks through those doors, looks around, and evaluates the effort it would take and the chances of a positive outcome, she makes the decision to continue with life as is. In her mind, "This won't work."

If you're one of the many "This won't work" leaders like Jocelyn, you're in great company. Many, many, many fall into this category. Unlike the "I got this" leader outlined above, the "This won't work" leader doesn't necessarily focus on his own value to the organization or the faucet of his knowledge spewing forth like a Slurpee machine. "This won't work" leaders may or may not have these tendencies, but more often than not, they are looking around at the people with whom they work and assessing the likelihood of real change, and saying, "Nah, not gonna happen."

Organizations are tough places, so there's certainly some legitimacy to the concerns of the "This won't work" leader. We hear them claim that there are too many organizational barriers to allow for a meaningful transformation. They often assert that historical precedent proves it can never happen there. This is often followed by the equally exasperated assessment, "We've tried that in the past, and it didn't work." Other reasons may include political limitations (uh, love and laughter work across the political divide), resource limitations (have you been paying attention? Love and laughter cost nothing), or time constraints (yeah, see above—love and laughter do not add time requirements).

"This won't work" leaders may also complain that people are the problem—those emotional carbon-based life forms that bring all their needs, wants, and desires to the workplace. Argh! In fact, that's what organizations are—groups of people—so we can't really get around this one. But cynical leaders are not to be deterred—they claim that their teams are to blame! And sometimes they are, but most times they're not. Perhaps it just takes a little attention to their needs to transform them from cubicle-campers to high performers. And while we always hope we have the most talented and driven teams around us, it doesn't always work that way. For every self-starter we may supervise, we can just as easily have three average or below-average performers. Such is life in the organization of today.

When all else fails, "This won't work" leaders will turn their gaze upward and blame those above. This may come in the form of "they," as in "They won't go for it. They won't listen. They tried this before." This mystical apparition has no form or frame. They are they. Any attempt to clarify who they are will be met with an immediate verbal exit strategy (e.g., "How 'bout them Dallas Cowboys?"). If we're really lucky, the "This won't work" leaders will zero in on the boss, and of course the fault lies therein. My boss will never go for this! My boss is results driven! My boss won't listen! The number of bad bosses out there, reportedly, is astronomical. OK, maybe, but maybe not.

Look, leaders like Jocelyn have a good point. Organizations that are unwilling to change, whether it's because of an overly comfortable workforce or disinterested supervisors, are a tough nut to crack. It is very difficult to implement change when the forces are stacked against you, but (not *and*) that is what leadership is all about. It is about making the decision to drive change instead of accepting the status quo. It begins with recognizing the barriers that need to be overcome.

"This Won't Work!" Barriers to Love and Laughter

It is true that leaders like Jocelyn are facing what seem to be insurmountable odds. Teams that are comfortable with the way things are, even if they are not happy, can slip into an operational neutral.

They achieve the goal of the company, but they don't reap the benefits of an environment that is marked by love and laughter. They know no better. Likewise, the bosses don't want to be bothered. Many of them may suffer from the all-knowing-leader mentality that we described before. This makes any significant organizational change even more challenging.

Still, it's not wise to let "This won't work" leaders off the hook so easily when they blame their misfortunes on those around them. Sometimes leaders like Jocelyn do not make the space for love and laughter in their workplace because they can't. Wait, no, that's not it. They think they can't. Their perception of what their teams and their bosses bring to the table doesn't give them the comfort level they need in order to take a shot at driving real organizational change. But perhaps the true source of the problem lies deeper within the "This won't work" leader. Most things do.

Those who attribute blame to others are often acting out of a need to project. Given the challenges of leading in today's complex business landscape and the near-constant risk of failure, who's to say? It would most certainly lend credence to the view that the "This won't work" leader is feeling badly that he personally cannot instill any significant change in his workplace, so the fault must lie elsewhere. This also enhances his sense of status in the group. If it's everyone else's fault, it must not be ours. We're the good ones; *they* are the bad ones. It's a terrific defense mechanism.

The organizational impact of this approach to leadership deserves special mention here. The word *stagnation* comes to mind. Or *cesspool*. When the "This won't work" leader refuses to accept responsibility for aggressively molding an organization, including with love and laughter, she is likely guilty of sins of omission in other areas as well—operations, production, or communication, to name a few.

Blaming others, even if the evidence is striking, is an abdication of leadership. It is the easiest way out for anyone who does not have the fortitude to drive change in an entity. The saddest aspect is that we can always influence someone! Admittedly, the impact may be limited to a small number of people under the direct supervision of the "This won't work" leader. But this is a start. This is how it begins. Even the slightest impact of bringing love and laughter into the workplace is worth the effort. Both love and laughter have a communicable nature to them. They grow quickly, and they spread quickly.

"This Won't Work!" Embracing Love and Laughter

Jocelyn has a great heart. She has identified something within her organization that needs attention, and she wants to do the right thing. Instead of looking around, noting the resistance in her midst, and backing away, she would be much better suited to embrace the opposition she faces. By doing so, she can identify strategic, incremental steps she can take to push her ideas forward. These will likely be bite-sized chunks of effort, but we're cool with that. Oh, and celebrate the success of each one!

When "This won't work" leaders meet with even modest success, good things happen. Laughter and love have a way of catching attention. When one division or department has embraced the tenets of humanity in the way they do their work, there is a palpable change in the vibe. Innovation, more efficient use of resources, and just plain fun become the norm. This gets noticed. When it does, people become curious. Everyone wants joy and happiness in their work, and the sad fact is that simply accomplishing the mission is not enough to ensure those pleasures. It never is. When we take the human out of the human who is performing the work, we are left with a robotic shell that does little more than what's necessary to stay employed. But going the opposite direction and embracing the aforementioned carbon-based life form, celebrating all that we bring, makes life fun.

Leaders like Jocelyn should also make a concerted effort to find like minds. There are many out there who, given even the slightest opening, would jump on the opportunity to make the workplace one of love and laughter. They often toil away quietly, knowing that their desired approach will be seen as soft and squishy and not strategically impactful. Identifying them through conversation or brown bag lunches or buying them a copy of our book (hint, hint) may be just enough to build the Love Force (as opposed to the Space Force—is that still a thing?) you need to make change.

Managing up becomes the order of the day if one faces senior leaders who are indifferent, as Jocelyn did. Sadly, this is more common in organizations than we would like to admit. Supervisors and executives, besieged by competitive and time pressures, may prove to be unlikely recipients of the love and laughter message. Simple and subtle approaches tend to work best in these situations, coupled with a strong *This is how this impacts you, boss* message. Dropping off an article you found interesting or mentioning a book you recently read may be all you need to plant the seed. If the work environment is one of trust, things get easier. A candid conversation will do the trick there.

Above all, for "This won't work" leaders to become "I'll make this work" leaders, they will have to be comfortable being patient, persistent, and resilient. This is no small task. We are an impatient society. A 24/7 news cycle, an internet always at the ready, and social platforms that beckon us to update the planet every time we blow our nose pressure us to want results now and switch to something else if we don't find them immediately. Sadly, organizational transformations don't work like that. They happen one smile at a time with love, inclusion, and tolerance. We have to keep trying, even if we don't see immediate change or naysayers abound.

We own the fact that organizational change is tough, and the task confronting the "This won't work" leader is significant. There's a lot of legitimacy to the challenges that our carbon-based forms introduce in the workplace. So, let's not be too hard on "This won't work" leaders. But let's not let them off the hook, either. We won't. Leadership is a responsibility. Go big or go home. By pushing beyond their comfort levels, even a small step at a time, "This won't work" leaders can instill love and laugher change in even the toughest environment.

It's All in the Mind

If at this point in the book you have come to the conclusion that we are being Pollyannaish, it may surprise you to know we aren't. We are not sticking our heads in the sand and ignoring the negative stuff. We are realists. (Incidentally, if you aren't aware of where the word *Pollyannaish* originates, it's from the work of Eleanor H. Porter, who penned a book in 1913 about a young girl named Pollyanna, who finds the positive in everything she faces. *She* should have taught leadership classes!) Actually, one of us is more Pollyannaish than the other and often gets accused (in a sweet way) of looking at the world through rose-colored glasses. It's not a bad way to approach life, just sayin'. But it would also be accurate to say we both have a cheerful and enthusiastic perspective on leadership.

Not everyone is like us, admittedly. There is no doubt that in all of our leadership journeys, we run into leaders who feel they know everything, and pursuing anything related to humor or compassion would be a nonstarter. We also encounter leaders who claim there is no point in pursuing positive change because their supervisors won't support it or their teams aren't interested.

Organizations can be better, and so can the leaders who lead them. Laughing and loving in our leadership practice can happen. It really can. Yes, the barriers are there but not insurmountable. Change is possible. We can, and should, drive our organizations to encompass the human aspect of leadership. When we let go and get real, we can make it happen. Our leaders can be better.

Are we positive psychologists? No, but we play them on television. In truth, we do subscribe to the tenets of positive psychology because we believe there is credence to the perspective that positivity is a constructive way to live. Productive too! It's easy to focus on the negative. Think about it for a moment. When we turn on the television or go to the internet, most of the time we find bad news. Psychologists suggest that this is due to the inherent negativity bias residing in our brain. The brain reacts much more swiftly to danger, and by incorporating the protective measures resulting from negativity bias, we are able to survive.

Negativity bias can also become addictive. As strange as it seems, we start to seek bad news. It becomes more salient to us, not only on television but in the workplace as well. This is buttressed by the neural pathways in our brain that contribute to our hereditary desire to be comfortable with the status quo. They nudge us toward those boring, predictable processes with which we've become accustomed. These are good when we need them but don't lend themselves well to a more accepting perspective, and certainly not to love and laughter. For that, it takes a more purposeful approach.

A downer mindset manifests itself in several ways. For example, we may blame ourselves whenever we hear bad news, automatically assuming responsibility for events that were probably out of our control, which reinforces the protective stance that we are prone to assume. This way of thinking also reveals itself when we anticipate bad news even before it occurs—yet another protective measure. We see this in the workplace when we make the assumption that a presentation we have worked very hard on will go wrong, no matter what we've done to prepare. Or when we assume that infusing a little love and laughter in our office will never work. If we fail, we don't feel as bad.

To be completely transparent, both of your authors suffer from one common aspect of negative thinking: we both tend to filter out positive feedback and focus solely on the bad stuff. Argh! For example, if either one of us receives a bad review for a speech or from a class that we've given, we tend to focus on that one poor review despite the fact that there may be several others that were very positive. We can't let it go! The rest of the day is ruined. Oh, my goodness, the number of times we've dealt with this, and the amount of Malbec we've consumed as a result! Oops, too much info?

Negative thinking not only can mess up an evening but also can have an undesirable physical impact. A pessimistic mindset has been shown to contribute to a decline in health as the grumpy person ages. A gloomy outlook is also associated with a weakened immune response, which leads to illness and infection. Is it worth it? Call us Pollyannaish, but we think not. Consider for a moment the alternative of embracing leadership through a more positive lens, one that assumes noble intent, seeks the best in people, and presents an optimistic view about the future. This is the domain of positive psychology, the one with which we find ourselves most attuned.

Positive psychology is a relatively new field of study. Having been around for only the last twenty-two or so years, it is an intriguing discipline whose basis is in the work of early humanists such as Carl Rogers, Mary Parker Follett, and Abraham Maslow. The emphasis is on the good that humans bring forth. Contrary to much work of early researchers who focused on mental illness, positive psychology is the study of happiness, and how to live a satisfying and fulfilling life.

Positive thinking is not Pollyannaish, despite the way we started this part of the book! Leaders with an encouraging outlook still hold nonperformers accountable for their work. They are still analytical, critical, and studied in their approaches to leadership. They drive change and are successful. The difference is in the outlook. When we interpret the world through a more affirmative lens, we tend to view those whom we work with and our work environments through a more positive lens as well. This helps us to create organizations of joy, laughter, and love. We are able to fashion environments where people feel engaged and where they trust one another. People are less likely to leave the organization and are more industrious. Creativity, passion, and productivity rule. Stressful situations are reduced to manageable occurrences where ingenuity is unleashed, and instead of curling into the proverbial ball during difficult times, people emerge as energetic and enthused.

Physically and psychologically, optimists fare far better than those with a more disconsolate outlook. Those with an encouraging attitude tend to be more balanced in their lives and are therefore able to deal with stress much more readily than their cynical counterparts.

They also prove to be healthier. For example, a positive mindset is associated with a healthier cardiovascular system and lower rates of depression. Researchers posit that this is due to a healthier lifestyle, more exercise, and a better life balance than what pessimists have. Regardless of the reason, we know that those with a positive outlook tend to resist common physical ailments more readily, due to a stronger immune response. They also live longer, and who wouldn't want that?

In today's world, full of tension and discord, showing the positive side of one's self is not the easiest thing to do. In the workplace, where the environment is cluttered with formalities and other organizational chaos, positivity may well get lost in the day-to-day goings on. Still, with a little focus and commitment, you can embrace this pathway, which opens the door to love and laughter in the workplace.

Start by making a conscious decision to steer away from the de-energizers. You know them. They suck the air out of a room when they arrive. Their mantra is "We can't, we don't." Likewise, avoid the negative thought patterns that pervade our brain and feed our negativity bias. Weigh the destructive contemplations you're having with the big picture. Is it worth it? Is it really that big of a deal? Will it be there later anyway? How much of it do you actually control?

You're now ready to wade into the world of positive thinking, a world that opens possibilities beyond the imagination. It is truly freeing. If you sense that negative thoughts are still wandering through your mind, that's OK. They have a tendency to do that, even in the most optimistic of souls. But by recognizing those negative pathways, you've taken the first and most crucial step in changing your mindset and your health.

Try positive self-talk. Positive thoughts have a way of feeding on themselves. Negative thoughts do as well. So, which one would you rather be consumed by? Ask yourself constructive questions about the situation you are facing: *What did I do well? What can I learn? How did this make a relationship better?* Close your eyes and create a vision of what you would like to see happen (no fair peeking). This exercises the imaginative portions of the brain and opens doors to prospective solutions. It relaxes you too. Not bad.

Finally, positivity opens the door to love. It allows us to laugh, and it's a demonstrably effective way to lead. Look at the evidence above, and in the first chapters. We are not claiming that love and laughter are a magic elixir (well, we are!). You will face doubters and cynics. You so will! Do you have the resolve? Is this a change you want to make? Are you willing? Is this a path you're prepared to travel? These are questions you must answer. Why?

Because it is now your choice.

CONCLUSION

I was traveling back home on a plane from the West Coast and found myself sitting in the aisle seat next to a gentleman in the middle seat who was an artist. Throughout the entire flight, he kept reaching down and grabbing sketchbooks and working on sketches that he had started probably many years before. At one point, I had to look over and let him know what beautiful work it was that he had produced. He told me he had not picked up a pencil to sketch, or brush to paint, until well after he retired. In fact, he was only two or three years into his life as an artist. Given the quality of his work, I was amazed at how beautiful his drawings and paintings were, especially for someone so new to art. I told him that he must be very proud to have such a wonderful talent. He said that much of what he was doing was sketching over the imperfections of his previous works. He described that in the sketches of Michelangelo and da Vinci, where they often went back to improve on the images that they had started sometimes years before. He pointed out the stray marks in previous works and asked me if I knew what they were. I responded that I did not. He told me they were previous images that had been sketched or painted over. What he was doing throughout this flight was going back and sketching over those flaws to improve the beauty of the image. In that moment, I learned a crucial lesson about self.

We are all imperfect human beings. We are all flawed. The goal is to continue to rebuild, rejuvenate, and rediscover ourselves throughout life. We refashion ourselves daily.

You are now at a decision point.

We will always face difficulty when we try to lead in the workplace. Sometimes these struggles will call into question our very values, what we stand for, and what we stand against. Likewise, we often face difficulty in life, outside of work. We don't always make the best decisions in our personal lives and often find ourselves in the position of having to adjust and readjust as we tackle the complexity of human life. We are simply works of art that get touch-ups all the time based on the humans we are and the humans we want to be. This is where you find yourself at this point in the book. What kind of leader do you want to be? What kind of human do you want to be?

From a work perspective, the facts are clear. We will always be more content with our "I got this" mentality. It gives us a sense of stability that allows for an artificial comfort. In our world of knowing everything, we reign, so all is well in the kingdom. And speaking of the kingdom, we consider our people to be fine, thank you! At least we think so. We also know that when faced with the challenge of driving change in an organization, we will have a tendency to default to the "This won't work" frame of mind. It makes it easier to blame others. Our bosses will never go for it. Our staff are set in their ways, or they just aren't up to such a daunting task. So, if this is the case, if it's truly hopeless, then we haven't reached you.

But we'd really like one final chance!

The evidence for love and laughter as an underpinning to our leadership is unequivocal. We know the impact it can have on an organization and on people. We know how it can make life better for other human beings. We also know it is not an easy thing to do. There will be naysayers, and there will be cynics. There will be people who roll their eyes and air-quote "soft skills" for you as they expose you to their diatribe of scripted methodology on what leadership is.

And we guarantee that there will be a dashboard! Yup, you will face enormous barriers.

It would be perfectly normal to have doubts. Self-doubt is common, and healthy. It detaches us from our comfort zone. If we don't doubt ourselves, we're not taking any risks. This means that whatever we're thinking about is important. Sometimes we will even fall into the vortex of need created by others, that flow of negative vibe where we get swept up on their path of self-loathing. Sorry, that was harsh! In truth, it's not those around us who own the blame for our unwillingness to embrace love and laughter. It's on us.

Self-doubt challenges us at a primal level. We like to be in control. But first we must begin with our venture into love and laughter. We must let go of that control we seek, let go of all the previous constructs we've leaned upon. We must tell our brain to step back from the contentment of artificial leadership paradigms until we get a handle on what truly makes us human. Isn't that more important?

We began this book by presenting the question as to why the shiny new approaches to leadership don't fill the gap. This scares us. Many of us spend our professional lifetimes focusing on leadership as an equation, a matrix, or a graphic. We spend time cloaked in the comfort that these creations provide. The answer is that some have value. They provide quick access to ideas and practices we may need to lean on as we face varied challenges in the workplace. But they have two main problems. First, they come with a price, the price of dependence. We tend to lean on these approaches as gospel, and straying too far from the script can leave us lost in the wilderness with nowhere to turn.

The second problem with these scripted models is that they rarely include anything related to basic human needs such as love or laughter. Some of the most well-known organizations that write reports each year extolling their approach to leadership never use the words *love*, *laugh*, *compassion*, *kindness*, *humor*, or *caring*. Trust us. We looked it up! The very humans that we are supposed to lead are treated like cogs in a wheel to be managed in accordance with a cookie-cutter approach (forgive the mixed metaphor). Good for robots, not for human beings. Let's return to Margaret again—a true story, by the way. Remember her from the introduction? She had all the right training and technically didn't do anything wrong. But she still struggled as a leader. So many of us do.

We hope that at this point you've reached a level of comfort with yourself where you will let go and get real. It will require you to make the connection between love and laughter. You will have to risk being a little vulnerable. You'll have to be self-aware. And then, we ask that you take that frightening leap into uncertainty. It's about getting real and diving into ourselves without reservation or judgment, but with curiosity. It requires us to be true to ourselves. It's about embracing a beginner's mind, with a childlike curiosity—one without the baggage of artificial constructs, preconceived assumptions, embedded beliefs, or false expectations.

We know you can do it. You can find the human in you and in others. You can feel love and have fun in your workplace. You can be a force for change in a complex landscape. You were born with all you need to lead, already embedded in your soul. Trust your desire to love. Trust your desire to laugh. You will make the world a better place.

REFERENCES

Aristotle and W. Rhys Roberts. 2004. *Rhetoric*. Mineola, NY: Dover Publications.

Barsade, S., and O. O'Neill. 2014a. "What's Love Got to Do with It? A Longitudinal Study of the Culture of Companionate Love and Employee and Client Outcomes in a Long-Term Care Setting." *Administrative Science Quarterly* 59, no. 4: 551–98.

Barsade, S., and O. O'Neill. 2014b. "Employees Who Feel Love Perform Better." *Harvard Business Review*. January 13.

Beard, Mary. 2014. *Laughter in Ancient Rome: On Joking, Tickling, and Cracking Up*. Oakland, CA: University of California Press.

Beddoes-Jones, F. 2017. "Love Is the Answer: A New Model of Corporate Love in the Workplace." Presentation at the British Psychological Society. http://www.fionabeddoesjones.com/resources.htm.

Berk, L., S. Tan, W. Fry, B. Napier, J. Lee, R. Hubbard, J. Lewis, and W. Eby. 1989. "Neuroendocrine and Stress Hormone Changes during Mirthful Laughter." *American Journal of the Medical Sciences* 298, no. 6: 390–96.

Berk, R. 2001. "The Active Ingredients in Humor: Psycho-physiological Benefits and Risks for Older Adults." *Educational Gerontology* 27: 323–39.

Bitterly B., and A. Brooks. 2020. "Sarcasm, Self-Deprecation, and Inside Jokes: A User's Guide to Humor at Work." *Harvard Business Review*. July–August.

Bitterly T. B., A. Brooks, and M. Schweitzer. 2017. "Risky Business: When Humor Increases and Decreases Status." *Journal of Personality and Social Psychology* 112, no. 3: 431–55.

Buchowski M., K. Majchrzak, K. Blomquist, K. Chen, D. Byrne, and J. Bachorowski. 2007. "Energy Expenditure of Genuine Laughter." *International Journal of Obesity* 31, no. 1: 131–37.

Chancellor, J., S. Margolis, K. Jacobs Bao, and S. Lyubomirsky. 2018. "Everyday Prosociality in the Workplace: The Reinforcing Benefits of Giving, Getting, and Glimpsing." *Emotion* 18, no. 4: 507–17.

Cheng, D., and L. Wang. 2014. "Examining the Energizing Effects of Humor: The Influence of Humor on Persistence Behavior." *Journal of Business and Psychology* 30, no. 4: 759–72.

Cigna. 2020. "Loneliness and the Workplace: 2020 U.S. Report." January.

Collins, Jim. 2001. *Good to Great: Why Some Companies Make the Leap . . . and Others Don't.* New York: HarperBusiness.

Cousins, Norman. 1979. *Anatomy of an Illness as Perceived by the Patient: Reflections on Healing and Regeneration.* New York: W. W. Norton.

Crompton, Dan. 2010. A Funny Thing Happened on the Way to the Forum: The World's Oldest Joke Book. London, UK: Michael O'Mara Books.

Derks, P., L. Gillikin, D. Bartolome-Rull, and E. Bogart. 1997. "Laughter and Electroencephalographic Activity." *Humor* 10, no. 3: 285–300.

Edmondson, Amy. 2019. *The Fearless Organization: Creating Psychological Safety in the Workplace for Learning, Innovation, and Growth.* Hoboken, NJ: John Wiley & Sons.

Fries, A., T. Ziegler, J. Kurian, S. Jacoris, and S. Pollak. 2005. "Early Experience in Humans Is Associated with Changes in Neuropeptides Critical for Regulating Social Behavior." *Proceedings of the National Academy of Sciences* 102, no. 47: 17237–40.

Gervais, M, and D. Wilson. 2005. "The Evolutions and Functions of Laughter and Humor: A Synthetic Approach." *Quarterly Review of Biology* 80, no. 4 (December): 395–430.

Hobbes, T. 1840. "Human Nature." In *The English Works of Thomas Hobbes of Malmesbury*, Vol. IV, edited by William Molesworth. London: John Bohn.

Holt-Lunstad, J., T. Smith, M. Baker, T. Harris, and D. Stephenson. 2015. "Loneliness and Social Isolation as Risk Factors for Mortality: A Meta-Analytic Review." *Perspectives on Psychological Science* 10, no. 2: 227–37.

Kant, Immanuel. 1951. *Critique of Judgment*. Translated by J. H. Bernard. New York: Hafner Publishing Co.

Konrath, S., E. O'Brien, and C. Hsing. 2010. "Changes in Dispositional Empathy in American College Students over Time: A Meta-Analysis." *Personality and Social Psychology Review* 15, no. 2: 180–98.

Krumrei-Mancuso, E. 2017. "Intellectual Humility and Prosocial Values: Direct and Mediated Effects." *Journal of Positive Psychology* 12, no. 1: 1–16.

Kuhn, C. 1994. "Stages of Laughter." *Journal of Nursing Jocularity* 4: 34–35.

Kurtz, L., and S. Algoe. 2017. "When Sharing a Laugh Means Sharing More: Testing the Role of Shared Laughter on Short-Term Interpersonal Consequences." *Journal of Nonverbal Behavior* 41, no. 1: 45–65.

Lewis, Thomas, Fari Amini, and Richard Lannon. 2000. *A General Theory of Love*. New York: Random House.

Louie, D., K. Brook, and E. Frates. 2016. "The Laughter Prescription: A Tool for Lifestyle Medicine." *American Journal of Lifestyle Medicine* 10, no. 4. 262–67.

Loye, David S. 2000. *Darwin's Lost Theory of Love: A Healing Vision for the 21st Century*. iUniverse.

McDonald, Paul. 2013. *The Philosophy of Humour (Philosophy Insights)*. Humanities E-books.

Men, Rita Linjuan. 2017. "It's About How Employees Feel! The Impact of Emotional Culture on Employee-Organization Relationships." Institute for Public Relations. July 23. https://instituteforpr.org/employees-feel-impact-emotional-culture-employee-organization-relationships.

Mesmer-Magnus, J., D. Glew, and C. Viswesvaran. 2012. "A Meta-Analysis of Positive Humor in the Workplace." *Journal of Managerial Psychology* 27, no. 2: 155–90.

Morreall, John, ed. 1987. The Philosophy of Laughter and Humor. Albany, NY: SUNY Press.

Myatt, Mike. 2012. "15 Ways to Identify Bad Leaders." *Forbes*. October 18. https://www.forbes.com/sites/mikemyatt/2012/10/18/15-ways-to-identify-bad-leaders/#60f3544715da.

Ou, A., D. Waldman, and S. Peterson. 2018. "Do Humble CEOs Matter? An Examination of CEO Humility and Firm Outcomes." *Journal of Management* 44, no. 3: 1147–73.

Palmer, Parker J. 2000. *Let Your Life Speak: Listening for the Voice of Vocation*. San Francisco, CA: Jossey-Bass.

Peck, M. Scott. 1978. *The Road Less Traveled: A New Psychology of Love, Traditional Values, and Spiritual Growth*. New York: Simon & Schuster.

Plato. 1926. *Laws: Books 7–12*. Translated by R. G. Bury. Boston: Harvard University Press.

Proto, E. 2016. "Are Happy Workers More Productive?" *IZA World of Labor*: 315. doi: 10.15185/izawol.315.

Provine, Robert R. 2000. *Laughter: A Scientific Investigation*. New York: Viking.

Shirom, A., S. Toker, Y. Alkaly, O. Jacobson, and R. Balicer. 2011. "Work-Based Predictors of Mortality: A 20-Year Follow-Up of Healthy Employees." *Health Psychology* 30, no. 3: 268–75.

Tarvin, Andrew. 2019. *Humor That Works: The Missing Skill for Success and Happiness at Work*. Page Two.

Treasurer, Bill. 2019. "The Three Types of Workplace Courage." *LeadingBlog*. May 5. https://www.leadershipnow.com/leadingblog/2019/05/the_three_types_of_workplace_c.html.

Urban Dictionary. 2008. "Jeep Wave." July 10.https://www.urbandictionary.com/define.php?term=Jeep%20Wave.

Varela-Silva, Inês. 2016. "Can a Lack of Love Be Deadly?" *The Conversation*. May 19. https://theconversation.com/can-a-lack-of-love-be-deadly-58659.

Yang, J., W. Zhang, and X. Chen. 2019. "Why Do Leaders Express Humility and How Does This Matter: A Rational Choice Perspective." *Frontiers in Psychology* 21 (August). https://doi.org/10.3389/fpsyg.2019.01925.

Zak, Paul J. 2017. *Trust Factor: The Science of Creating High-Performance Companies*. New York: American Management Association.

Zauderer, D. 2002."Workplace Incivility and the Management of Human Capital." *Public Manager* (Spring): 36–42.

INDEX

ABOUT THE AUTHORS

Zina Sutch and Patrick Malone

Zina Sutch was born and grew up in New England, where she earned her bachelor's degree in business and economics from Clark University, in Massachusetts. She enjoyed spending her leisure hours in Boston and New York until she moved to the Washington, DC, area to pursue her master's degree in special education from George Washington University. While working in the field of education, she earned her PhD from the University of Maryland studying behavioral disorders. She believes this is why she can pretty much get along with everybody, especially Patrick. She taught in public and private schools and served as the director of a private school for students with emotional and behavioral disorders before joining the federal government and leading development and diversity programs in the Senior Executive Service. Currently, while continuing in the Senior Executive Service, she is a faculty member in the Key Executive Leadership Program in the School of Public Affairs at American University teaching courses on leadership, team building, and succession planning.

Patrick Malone was born and grew up in Texas. He enjoyed his leisure hours in Austin while earning his bachelor's degree at Texas State University studying health care administration. After graduating and working as a surgical technician, he moved to San Antonio to complete his master's degree at Trinity University, followed by work in the private sector health care industry. He then joined the Navy and served as a hospital administrator in the Medical Service Corps, also earning his PhD in public administration and American government from the School of Public Affairs at American University. After a twenty-three-year naval career, he joined the faculty at American University as an executive in residence and now serves as the director of the Key Executive Leadership Programs.

And there's the connection! Zina and Patrick met while at American University, where they not only found that they had a lot in common with respect to their histories but also discovered that they shared similar values, even though they had grown up in two very different parts of the country. Both believed in the same principles when it came to leadership development, social science takeaways, and common human decency. As they spent more and more time together talking and getting to know each other, they realized that together they could do more than either could do on their own. They still believe that there is so much more to learn and share, and they plan to continue exploring new ideas and new ways to uncover the leader within each unique individual.

Zina and Patrick live on the Chesapeake Bay, Maryland, on a forty-foot Bavaria Vision sailboat. Never having sailed, they accepted an invitation to sail with friends and decided that this was the life they wanted, on the water, learning something new about sailing, themselves, and each other almost every day. Without knowing how to sail, or what anything on the sailboat was called (which is really, really complicated), they made the leap, purchased the boat, and aptly named it *Madness*. There is more to the boat name, but those stories are for a different time!

Berrett-Koehler is an independent publisher dedicated to an ambitious mission: *Connecting people and ideas to create a world that works for all.*

Our publications span many formats, including print, digital, audio, and video. We also offer online resources, training, and gatherings. And we will continue expanding our products and services to advance our mission.

We believe that the solutions to the world's problems will come from all of us, working at all levels: in our society, in our organizations, and in our own lives. Our publications and resources offer pathways to creating a more just, equitable, and sustainable society. They help people make their organizations more humane, democratic, diverse, and effective (and we don't think there's any contradiction there). And they guide people in creating positive change in their own lives and aligning their personal practices with their aspirations for a better world.

And we strive to practice what we preach through what we call "The BK Way." At the core of this approach is *stewardship,* a deep sense of responsibility to administer the company for the benefit of all of our stakeholder groups, including authors, customers, employees, investors, service providers, sales partners, and the communities and environment around us. Everything we do is built around stewardship and our other core values of *quality, partnership, inclusion,* and *sustainability.*

This is why Berrett-Koehler is the first book publishing company to be both a B Corporation (a rigorous certification) and a benefit corporation (a for-profit legal status), which together require us to adhere to the highest standards for corporate, social, and environmental performance. And it is why we have instituted many pioneering practices (which you can learn about at www.bkconnection.com), including the Berrett-Koehler Constitution, the Bill of Rights and Responsibilities for BK Authors, and our unique Author Days.

We are grateful to our readers, authors, and other friends who are supporting our mission. We ask you to share with us examples of how BK publications and resources are making a difference in your lives, organizations, and communities at www.bkconnection.com/impact.

Dear reader,

Thank you for picking up this book and welcome to the worldwide BK community! You're joining a special group of people who have come together to create positive change in their lives, organizations, and communities.

What's BK all about?

Our mission is to connect people and ideas to create a world that works for all.

Why? Our communities, organizations, and lives get bogged down by old paradigms of self-interest, exclusion, hierarchy, and privilege. But we believe that can change. That's why we seek the leading experts on these challenges—and share their actionable ideas with you.

A welcome gift

To help you get started, we'd like to offer you a **free copy** of one of our bestselling ebooks:

www.bkconnection.com/welcome

When you claim your **free ebook**, you'll also be subscribed to our blog.

Our freshest insights

Access the best new tools and ideas for leaders at all levels on our blog at ideas.bkconnection.com.

Sincerely,

Your friends at Berrett-Koehler